GUIDE TO CUBAN
GENEALOGICAL RESEARCH
Records and Sources

I0100039

PETER E. CARR

CLEARFIELD

Originally published
San Bernardino, California, 1991

Reprinted for
Clearfield Company, Inc. by
Genealogical Publishing Co., Inc.
Baltimore, Maryland
2000

International Standard Book Number: 0-8063-5028-8

Made in the United States of America

To
Boss

Abbreviations

```
AGI    = Archivo General de Indias, Seville, Spain
AHN    = Archivo Historico Nacional, Madrid, Spain
ANC    = Archivo Nacional de Cuba, C.Habana, Cuba
BNC    = Biblioteca Nacional "Jose Marti", C.Habana,
           Cuba
CSt-H  = California State Univ., Hayward
CU     = University of California, Berkeley
D.C.   = District of Columbia, U.S.A.
DLC    = Library of Congress, Washington, D.C.
FL     = Florida
FMU    = University of Miami
ft.    = feet
FU     = University of Florida, Gainesville
Imp.   = Imprenta (press or printer)
LDS    = Latter-Day Saints
MA     = Massachusetts
MB     = Boston Public Library
MD     = Maryland
MH     = Harvard University, Cambridge, MA
n/a    = not applicable or not available
NC     = North Carolina
NcU    = University of North Carolina
n.d.   = no date
NN     = New York Public Library
Ntra.  = Nuestra
Pres.  = Presidente (President)
SC     = South Carolina
Sra.   = Señora
UCLA   = University of California, Los Angeles
VA     = Virginia
```

ACKNOWLEDGEMENTS

This book could not and would not have been written were it not for the prodding and encouragement of my mother, Carmen. She had to put up with a messy living room for an incredibly long time while I compiled and wrote this book. Many times, when it seemed as if it would not become a reality, she offered her advice and very constructive criticism.

Equally so, my niece Aimee supplied me with countless words of love and affection which made me persevere during very difficult times. The use of her massive, roll-top desk provided a place of quiet where I could concentrate on my task.

I would like to thank my father, Pedro, for all the knowledge and details he provided. His undying devotion to Cuba was an inspiration.

Moreover, a heartfelt "THANKS" goes to all the family members who helped, but who have since gone to their rest. I owe a debt of gratitude to living family members in Cuba who encouraged and helped me even while having to cope with their lives under a despotic, phony and terrorist regime.

Lastly, but certainly not least, I would like to thank Chris KNIGHT for his expert computer help. Hermez MORENO is very deserving of a word of gratitude for always being there. However, without the "shove" which my friend Julio VERA gave me, I doubt if I ever would have finished this book. The sustinence which his wife, Kukla, and daughters, Helen and Maria, provided gave me energy beyond belief.

Highland, California   Peter E. Carr
10 October 1991

v

TABLE OF CONTENTS

INTRODUCTION

The necessity for a comprehensive guide to Cuban genealogical research is long overdue. This need notwithstanding, the principal obstacle to obtaining genealogical records and materials from Cuba remains its own repressive government. This is especially true if one resides in the United States or any other non-communist nation which does not have diplomatic ties with Cuba.

The animosity of the Cuban government towards the United States is a real hindrance. Additionally, American embargo laws make it illegal to obtain any information or records from Cuba which require a payment. However, it is not impossible to obtain documents, even when no monetary transaction takes place. Though this may exclude most governmental records, there a vast amount of other sources available, especially from the Catholic Church. The matter of compensation, if any, to each church is left to the individual researcher as it is not absolutely necessary.

Over the past twenty five years, the author has been accumulating records and sources related to Cuba throughout the world. These resources allow one to circumvent some of the obstacles presented. A considerable amount of worthwhile research may be done by using the sources outside of Cuba. While many of these resources are considered to be secondary in nature, their value is incalculable. This is especially true if one wishes to create a family history and not just a family tree. After all, genealogy is about the lives and times of individuals and families and not just about their names and vital statistics.

Though limited by access problems, this guide will help the persistent genealogist locate and use many lesser known resources which are within relatively easy reach of someone outside of Cuba. These resources will allow the genealogist to answer the four basic genealogical questions—who, what, when and where.

One does not have to have famous or well-known ancestors to find them in a myriad of documents and publications. This guide, though far from complete,

1

is written as a base from which one may progress in their research. A simple fact, such as locating a relative in a city directory, may lead one to many other records, if one knows where to search.

It must be kept in mind that correspondence with the Catholic Church in Cuba is not prohibited, neither in the United States, Spain, or England nor in Cuba. However, one must always respect the fear under which the people in Cuba always live. Equally so, their lack of resources, such as photocopy machines, may be frustrating to the genealogist, but it is nothing compared to the suffering of the Cuban people under the system of misrule which presently pervades Cuba.

Lastly, one must be mindful that if those of us outside of Cuba have difficulties communicating with anyone in Cuba, then, by the same token, those in Cuba have similar or worse problems of communication.

PRELIMINARY RESEARCH

The difficulties encountered while researching one's Cuban ancestors may be lessened considerably by proper preparation and planning with living relatives, available records and other information.

A preliminary survey of available documents in the home should be done in order to pinpoint precisely where in Cuba one needs to pursue the investigation.

When reviewing any type of document, the names of the godparents, witnesses and other individuals present ay any event, should not be ignored. These may provide valuable clues which may lead the genealogist to further records.

A secondary review of the documentation should be done after the investigation has begun and is in the preliminary stages. Many times, additional details are noticed based on the newly-found records. A periodic review of home documents may yield additional clues.

When researching a family from La Habana or Havana, Santiago de Cuba or another of the larger cities, one needs to pinpoint the address as much as possible. This is a necessity because of the larger number of parishes and municipal districts present within the cities.

Using city directories, military records and even newspaper advertisements, one may be able to ascertain a precise location. Bear in mind that a great many people went outside of their respective parishes for a baptism or marriage. This situation is the type where one needs to apply the concept of family history as often research on a collateral line may yield valuable information to break an impasse on a direct line.

To help in determining dates, that is, the day and month of an event such as a baptism, the names of the persons involved may be very helpful. Since Cuba was a predominantly Catholic country, the custom was, as in Spain, to give the newly-born child at least one of the names of the saints whose feast was being commemorated on the day of his birth.

3

This custom, when combined with the names of the ancestors, sometimes brought about incredibly long names such as Pedro Emilio Juan Climaco Pastor Osvaldo Manuel CARR y RODRIGUEZ. Pedro Emilio was taken from the father while Osvaldo and Manuel were from both grandfathers. The remaining names, Juan, Climaco and Pastor, were the names of the saints whose feastday was being celebrated on the date of birth.

It must be kept in mind that the calendar of saints of the Catholic Church has varied and changed many times throughout its history. So, when applying this concept, one needs to locate the proper calendar for the era in question.

Occupations may also be useful in determining an address in one of the larger Cuban cities. For some reason, each different trade or type of merchant tended to congregate in a particular area or street. For example, in La Habana many tailors were found along Calle (street) Obispo, fabric stores along Calle Muralla, along the Calzada (causeway) de Galiano large department stores opened their shops and the Manzana de Gomez (Gomez Block) was full of men's clothing stores.

During the 19th century and earlier, the owners of these shops lived nearby or upstairs of the shop. Sometimes, the living quarters were a couple of small rooms plus a bathroom and kitchen in the rear of the building housing the business.

One very good source of much information is the older generation. This resource is sometimes neglected because the researcher feels that older people have forgotten much of their early lives or that it is a bother to them. Although the very specifics may have been forgotten or some accomplishments enhanced, our grandparents and great-grandparents may be able to provide important clues which may help solve seemingly impossible problems.

The closeness of the Cuban family and the fact that life in Cuba was lived in extended homes containing several generations are assets which should be exploited.

Additionally, older folks are usually glad to help and share what they have. This sharing makes

4

them feel that they are contributing and leaving a part of themselves behind. Indeed, they are! However, one needs to realize that the energy level of an older person may be limited, though not always so. Therefore, it may be necessary to talk with them several times in order to gather as much information as possible while meeting their energy requirements.

Everything, no matter how seemingly trivial it may appear, should be written down or recorded on tape. Even an insignificant story may yield valuable information later on. Periodically, as the research progresses, one needs to do follow-up interviews with the older relatives. This second or later interview serves the dual purpose of keeping them abreast of new finds which may in turn trigger memories of events previously unrecalled.

A family historian should always attempt to provide as complete a picture as possible of their ancestors and their lives. To this end, all tape recordings or videos made should be saved for posterity. A safe and environmentally sound place is necessary for their storage. A bank safety deposit box serves this purpose very well.

SURNAME VERSUS LAST NAMES

Many times confusion arises when Spanish or Hispanic surnames are being researched. This confusion arises from the fact that Hispanic people usually have and use two surnames.

Additional confusion stems from the fact that some researchers base their investigations on last names instead of surnames. Many times I have seen a publication which contains Hispanic surnames indexed by the second of these only! In this way, unless the reader encounters the first surname in the text, it cannot be easily located, if at all.

Though this may appear to be a matter of semantics, genealogically speaking, it is most incorrect. This is because the name written last (from which the term "last name" originated) may not be the person's only surname. The correct term and concept is either "surname" or "family name" with which it is somewhat synonymous.

As previously stated, most people of Spanish heritage have and use at least two surnames. Some have more than two. This is the case for those whose family names consist of compound surnames as in HURTADO DE MENDOZA which has become to be considered one surname. This or any other compound surname, when combined with a simple or another compound surname, can lead to very long surnames.

The method by which a child acquires two surnames is simple. The first surname is taken from the father's first surname while the second surname is acquired from the mother's first surname.

For example, a man named Blas MEDEROS SARMIENTO marries Lucia PEREZ RAMOS and they have a daughter. They name her Clara and her surnames are then MEDEROS PEREZ. The "y" which is sometimes in between two surnames as in Maria Luisa RENCURRELL y PELLARD is not part of the surname. It is only the conjunction "and" linking the two surnames.

In Hispanic societies, there is no usage of the mother's first surname as a middle or second name of an offspring as happens in Anglo-Saxon or other European cultures. This happens very, very,

6

rarely in Hispanic cultures. So if one encounters a person with the surnames of DIAZ RODRIGUEZ, it may be safely assumed that the father was surnamed DIAZ and the mother RODRIGUEZ and not vice versa.

This dual system of surnames works well and is easy to follow and trace. However, from the middle of the 19th century back, the system is fuzzy and becomes somewhat complicated.

The main reason for this complication is that women use one set of surnames and men another. The example taken from the marriage in 1608 between Gabriel GONZALEZ DE LA MOTA and Maria XIMENEZ (modern JIMENEZ) illustrates this very well. In 1612, they have a daughter, Maria, who subsequently has been found in records as Maria XIMENEZ DE LA MOTA, Maria DE LA MOTA and Maria GONZALEZ DE LA MOTA. Never is she found as Maria GONZALEZ XIMENEZ as one would expect if using the modern surname system. She is found most frequently as Maria XIMENEZ DE LA MOTA while all her male siblings are found as GONZALEZ DE LA MOTA.

It is evident from the above example tha males as a rule were given both of the father's surnames without any regard for the surnames of the mother. At the same time, females, without much variation, were given as their first surname their mother's first surname and not their father's.

Females usually acquired their second surname from the father's second surname. Moreover, females were usually known by one surname instead of two. During these ancient times, one may find generation after generation of mothers and daughters with the same surnames and without any indication of the fathers' surnames.

At this time, clarification is necessary regarding the English and American systems of "Mrs." and the Hispanic "Señora" (abbreviated "Sra.") and the "de" designations.

In the Anglo-Saxon world, if one finds a record which names a Mrs.John SMITH, one knows that it refers to John's wife. However, with this type of designation her proper name and surname are not given. Additionally, John's wife will use his surname as hers. Her maiden surname, unless mentioned,

7

remains unknown from then on.

However, in Hispanic societies, this system is very rarely, if ever, used. The genealogist is not likely to find a record for Sra.Juan PEREZ GARCIA. Likewise, a woman named Maria DELGADO GUTIERREZ will not become Maria PEREZ GARCIA if she marries Juan. She never takes her husband's surname as her own. This is an erroneous assumption made by many unfamiliar with Spanish culture and surname usage.

The ways used to designate that a Hispanic woman is married are simple. Either she is known as Sra.Carmen PITA MEDEROS, PITA AND MEDEROS being her birth surnames and not her husband's, or, if she marries Manuel LUACES DIAZ, then she may be known as Carmen PITA MEDEROS "de" LUACES. The word "de" meaning literally, "of".

At times, she may even be known as Sra.de LUACES which is similar, but not exactly the same, as Mrs.SMITH. If the husband's surname happens to already have the preposition "de" as in DE MARTINEZ, one would still write an additional "de" when designating the wife, i.e., DE DE MARTINEZ. Literally, translating to "of of MARTINEZ.

In Hispanic genealogical research, it is very desirable to research the origins of a surname in order to avoid confusion. This is especially true when researching in the 15th century or earlier. As an example, the surname SOTOMAYOR had its origins with the surnames of SORREZ, SORREZ FERNANDEZ and FERNANDO or FERRAN sometime in the 7th century, although in Spain surnames were not in common use until approximately the 11th century.

A very good source for the origins of Spanish surnames is the <u>Diccionario Heraldico y Genealogico de Apellidos Españoles y Americanos</u> by Alberto and Arturo GARCIA CARRAFFA. This vast work was published in Madrid, Spain during the 1950s. It consists of 88 volumes and each surname has an extensive bibliography which may be used for further research. Its one drawback is that the GARCIA CARRAFFA brothers were not able to finish it and so it ends with the letter U. It is readily available in libraries throughout the United States, Spanish America and Europe.

In early times, Spanish surnames were very interchangable and sometimes the mother's surname was placed first instead of second. Another peculiarity is brought about by patronymic surnames.

Patronymic surnames are those derived from the father's proper name such as ALVAREZ from Alvaro, FERNANDEZ from Fernando and GARCIA from Garci. As an example, about the 14th century there was a man named Garci MENDEZ DE SOTOMAYOR who married Teresa FERNANDEZ DE SAAVEDRA. They had two children. The first was a girl named Mencia GARCIA DE SOTOMAYOR and the other was a boy named Alonso GARCIA DE SOTO MAYOR. Note that in both cases the surname became GARCIA DE SOTOMAYOR instead of MENDEZ DE SOTOMAYOR.

The GARCIA portion was derived from the father Garci. Subsequently, Mencia marries Ferran PEREZ BARROSO and their descendants use the BARROSO surname and not PEREZ. Meantime, Alonso marries Urraca PEREZ BARROSO and their son is anmed Garci MENDEZ DE SOTOMAYOR. Obviously, he was named for the paternal grandfather and so the GARCIA has disappeared while MENDEZ has reappeared.

A word of caution must be added regarding the spelling of Spanish surnames. As with other cultures, it is only within the last 150 to 200 years that the spelling of Hispanic surnames has become standardized. So it is not surprising to find early records with such surnames as SOTOMAYOR spelled as SOTOMAIOR or even SOTOMALLOR.

1492 — On the night of 27 October and early morning of the 29th, the island called Cuba by its native population was sighted by Christopher COLUMBUS' vessels during his first voyage to the New World. COLUMBUS named the island Juana, but by Royal Decree of 1515, it was renamed Fernandina. However, neither name persisted for very long and it remained known as Cuba instead.

1512 — Baracoa, the first Cuban town, was founded along the northeast coast by Diego VELAZQUEZ.

1513 — Bayamo is founded on the eastern portion of the island.

1514 — Santiago de Cuba, Trinidad and Sancti Spiritus were founded on the eastern portion. San Cristobal de La Habana was founded on the south coast of the western portion.

1519 — San Cristobal is transferred to the northern side of the island to a place know previously as Puerto (port) de Carenas. Henceforth, it becomes known as Havana, Habana, or La Habana.

1520 — Obispado (bishopric) de Cuba is created by the Catholic Church. Its seat was in Santiago de Cuba which in its early days was simply known as Cuba.

1536 — From approximately this year, all "realengos" (Royal Lands) were officially distributed by the "merced" system. That is, the land was given to individuals out of "mercy". They held title in usufruct, but did not actually own the land. This system lasted until 1729.

1553 — La Habana is named capital of Cuba.

1592 — By Royal Decree, La Habana was elevated from a "villa" (village or town) to a city. By the end of the century, it had a hospital as well as an aqueduct. Sugar began its prominence in the economy of Cuba at this time.

1607 — The government is divided into two branches.
The one in La Habana is responsible for the
western portion of the island under the com-
mand "Capitan General" (Captain General) of
Cuba. The government in Santiago de Cuba is
responsible for that city plus Bayamo, Baracoa and Puerto del Principe (later known as
Puerto Principe and still later Camaguey).
The commander was the "Capitan de Guerra" or
Captain of War. An oversight occurred in the
towns named and which government had juris-
diction and so Trinidad, Sancti Spiritus and
El Cano or La Sabana (modern Remedios in a
different location) were left as independent
entities to fend for themselves. As soon as
the error was noticed it was corrected.

1621 — La Habana is hit by an epidemic of malaria.

1637 — La Habana is hit by epidemics of small pox
and measles.

1649 — An epidemic of yellow fever kills one third
of the population of La Habana.

1651 — Bubonic plague spreads throughout La Habana
and the nearby region.

1653 — Santiago de Cuba and Bayamo suffer through
an epidemic of yellow fever.

1664 — A major hurricane destroys over 200 houses
in La Habana.

1677 — Several epidemics hit La Habana at once. The
to   small pox epidemic continues after many of
1686   the others have abated.

1692 — A major hurricane wreaks havoc on the La Habana area. In Guanabacoa, the parish church
and "Cabildo"(council) house are demolished.

1695 — Santiago de Cuba is devastated by a yellow
fever epidemic.

1701 — The Spanish War of Succession takes place
to   after which the government of Cuba becomes
1714   more centralized and directly controlled by
the Crown. Tobacco farming becomes prominent
at this time.

11

1722   In Santiago de Cuba,the first institution of
        of higher learning in Cuba is started.

1728 — The Universidad de La Habana is founded.

1733 — The island's government is centralized in La
        Habana.

1740 — Spanish and English War during which Cuba
to   was briefly attacked by England, especially
1748   in the Guantanamo area. By mid-18th century
        almost all of the shops of shoemakers, car-
        penters, plumbers, tailors and other trades
        owned by free black people known as "negros
        horros".

1756 — The first postal system on the island is put
        into service.

1762 — A British army invades La Habana and the ci-
to   ty capitulates on the 12th of August. The
1763   Spanish capital of Cuba is transferred to
        Santiago de Cuba. The civil administration
        of La Habana is left in local Spanish hands
        with the British commanding officer as its
        head. The Treaty of Versailles ends the war
        between Spain, France and England. La Haba-
        na is returned to Spanish control on the 6th
        of July 1763. This brief English occupation
        had an influence on the burgeoning indepen-
        dence movements on the island. The American
        Revolution and, especially the French Revol-
        ution, also contributed to the separatist
        rumblings. As part of the terms of the Tre-
        aty, Spain ceded Florida to the English. A
        large migration of Spanish families to Cuba
        ensued.

1767 — The expulsion of the Jesuits takes place.

1771 — Marques DE LA TORRE becomes the Captain Gen-
to   eral of Cuba and brings about many public
1776   works with the help of the citizenry. Many
        new bridges, theaters and towns are built.

1778 — Commerce between Spain and the West Indies
        is liberalized.

1787 — La Sociedad Economica de Amigos del Pais is
        founded in Santiago de Cuba by intellectuals

and merchants. Its goal is to promote agriculture, commerce and the education of the Cuban youth. This society begins in La Habana. in 1793.

1799 – Thousands of French begin migrating to Cuba from Haiti and settle in Santiago de Cuba and the surrounding area. These immigrants start many coffee plantations which become a thriving business.

1800 – The "Audiencia (court) de Santo Domingo" is transferred to Puerto Principe due to the Revolution. This allows Cuban citizens greater access to this court making it easier to appeal cases.

1802 – Many French and Spanish families migrate to Cuba from Louisiana.

1808 – In March of this year, any French immigrant who has not become a Spanish citizen is expulsed from Cuba. his occurred because of the war between Spain and Napoleon and questioned French loyalties.

1818 – Cuba's commerce is now mainly with foreign markets in England and the United States instead of with Spain.

1819 – A Royal Decree grants actual ownership of the land previously given by "merced". If no documentary evidence for the land grant could be furnished,then proof of having possessed and worked the land for the prior 40 years was sufficient to gain permanent ownership.

1821 – Legal importation of slaves partially abolished by a pact between Spain and England. By 1834, it becomes a total abolition of the importation of new slaves. However,this does not eliminate the ownership nor the illegal importation of slaves. The independence of Mexico causes the migration of many Spanish families to Cuba from Mexico.

1821 – The independist conspiracy called "Soles y
to   Rayos de Bolivar" takes place. Their goal is
1823   to establish the Republic of Cubanacan. Its

13

failure causes most of the conspirators and their families to flee to United States and Mexico. The most popular migration places in the United States are New York, Philadelphia and New Orleans.

1827 – Administratively, the island is divided into three departments: Occidental, Central and Oriental. The Occidental Department was composed of the (1959) provinces of Pinar del Rio (formerly Nueva Filipina and Vuelta Abajo), La Habana, Matanzas and Las Villas. The central department was made up by Camaguey. The Oriental Department consisted of the Oriente province. Bear in mind tha Cuba had many subdivisions. These were ecclesiastic, administrative, military, territorial, political, maritime, judicial and several other minor ones.

1833 – A great cholera epidemic sweeps the island and causes many deaths, especially in its western portion. For a general review of the great mortality see,"Resumen general que manifiesta los cadaveres colericos sepultados en los cementerios de esta ciudad y sus extramuros y en las diferentes poblaciones de la Isla desde el 25 de febrero ultimo hasta el 30 de septiembre inclusivo (1833)". This document is located in the Archivo Historico Nacional (AHN), Madrid, Estado section,legajo (bundle) 6374, document 81.

1839 – The "Audiencia de La Habana" is created.

1842 – The first public schools are created island-wide.

1851 – In this year, the military division of Cuba consists of one Captaincy General made up of a western and an eastern department.

1853 – Destruction of the city wall of La Habana is started. It continued slowly until only a few pieces remained standing at the start of the 20th century.

1857 – A yellow fever epidemic causes havoc in La Habana.

1868 - On the 10th of October,Carlos Manuel DE CES-
       PEDES started the first island-wide war   for
       independence.   Many people   emigrated   from
       Cuba to the United States, especially to Key
       West, Tampa, New Orleans, New York City   and
       Philadelphia. After January 1869, the migra-
       tion reached epic proportions due to the
       fact that the Spanish "Voluntarios"(army vo-
       lunteers) went on a rampage of terrorist ac-
       tivities against suspected of aiding the Cu-
       ban cause. By the end of 1869, over 100,000
       people had left the island. The war ended in
       what was basically an armistice and no reso-
       lution of the independence question.

1879 - On 1 January, the island is divided into six
       provinces. They are the same as   the   1959
       provinces except for Camaguey which is still
       called Puerto Principe.

1886 - Slavery is completely abolished in Cuba.

1891 - Reciprocity agreement between Cuba   and   the
       United States which assures   Cuba's leading
       position in the world sugar market.

1895 - On the 24th of February, Cuba's War of Inde-
       pendence begins. Again, there is much   emi-
       gration from the island to United States and
       Mexico.

1898 - On the 15th of February,the American battle-
       ship Maine explodes and sinks in the   harbor
       of La Habana. This gives rise to the   Span-
       ish-American War. Although the fighting ends
       in August, the war does not   officially   end
       until the 10th of December when   the   Treaty
       of Paris is signed.

1899 - On the 1st of January, the island of Cuba as
       well as other Spanish possessions are turned
       over to the   United   States   administration.
       The first American intervention begins   with
       General John R. BROOKE as the first Military
       Governor.

1902 - On the 20th of May, the American   occupation
       ends and Cuba becomes an independent   repub-
       lic.

1906 — On the 29th of September, the second American
       intervention begins with William H. TAFT as
       Provisional Governor.

1909 — On the 28th of January, the Cuban Republic is
       restored.

1959 — After decades of mismanagement and corrupt-
       tion, Fidel CASTRO deposes the cowardly dic-
       tator Fulgencio BATISTA. First viewed as a
       hero, CASTRO shortly shows his true colors,
       or color, and institutes a Communist form of
       government. Under the guise of the "revolu-
       tion" he sets about to systematically destroy
       Cuba and her people. Intellectuals who do
       not have to go through the suffering of dai-
       ly life on the island, praise the "revolu-
       tion" for its great strides in medicine and
       education. Most of the world's press are ta-
       ken in by the regime's propaganda machine as
       they report of the wonderful "revolution".
       Needless to say, that a large migration of
       Cubans from all walks of life takes place.
       The bulk going to the United States, Spain
       and Mexico.

CHURCH RECORDS

Being a predominantly Catholic nation,the bulk
of church records are those kept by the different
parish churches throughout the island. This is especially significant when one considers that up until the time that civil registration commenced,any-
one that wanted to be legally married in Cuba, had
to do so in the Catholic Church.

If one was not Catholic, either the marriage
had to have taken place prior to arriving in Cuba,
or the couple could be married at the consulates of
another country. However, this service was usually
reserved for the citizens of the particular nation.

Additionally, a couple could travel to a nearby predominantly Protestant country and marry in
any one of the many Protestant denominations available in those places. St. Paul's Episcopal Church
in Key West, Florida was one of the popular ones
for those living in La Habana because of the ease
of access.

Another restriction usually circumvented by
travelling outside of Cuba was that imposed on a
woman if she became a widow. This restriction made
the woman wait at least two years to remarry.

One should not be surprised if a record cannot
be located. Many of the poorer people could not pay
the fees charged by the officiating priests.

For example, during the 1820s and 1830s, the
charge for a baptism was about 6 reales or approximately 75 cents. By the 1860s, the charge had risen
to one dollar and upwards. By the 1870s, the "upwards meant up to $17.00 depending on the church
and ceremony.

Burials were not cheap either. The cost was
anywhere from five to seven and a half dollars. The
difference in the price was due to the amount of
pomp and circumstance of the ceremony as well as
amount of verbiage by the priest.

The following is a list of the charges made by
the Catholic Church for different services during
the decade of the 1850s:

Baptism	1 peso
Free adult burial	7.5 pesos
Free child burial	6.5 pesos
Slave adult burial	5.5 pesos
Slave child burial	5 pesos
For each prayer stop en route to the cemetery	12.5 pesos
For sung High Mass	6 pesos
For high cross at the burial	2 pesos
For marriage	7.5 pesos
For marriage ceremony at home (in addition to marriage fee)	4 pesos
For non-resident certification	25 pesos
Any certification (for residents)	1 peso

This list was published by Garcia de Arboleya.

While these prices may not seem so high in our day and age, bear in mind that the average person in those days was not making more than about 100 pesos a year, if that. However, if any person was too poor and could not afford to pay, they were not charged.

In November of 1563, the Council of Trent in Italy reached an accord whereby each parish church was to keep registers of baptisms, confirmations, marriages and burials. Most of these records are still available from the local parish churches in Cuba.

There are many books available which may help determine the parish at which an event may have taken place. Juan Martin Leiseca's Apuntes para la Historia Eclesiastica de Cuba published in La Habana in 1938 gives the history of each parish then in existence and its location.

This publication also contains a somewhat detailed history of the Catholic Church in Cuba. It has an unpaged appendix called, "Paginas de Honor", which provides much biographical data of many different people. Photographs of many of them are also shown. All data given on these people is prior to 1938 and some of it goes back to the 19th century.

Other books, such as the Guia Geografica y Administrativa de la Isla de Cuba by Pedro J. Imberno published in La Habana in 1891 and the various Guia de Forasteros provide lists of parishes and their locations. After locating the probable parish for an event, it is then a simple matter of writing a letter in Spanish requesting the record. The name of the person, the type of event and a very approximate time period should be provided. The letter may be addressed to: Parroquia de (insert name of church at this point), name of town or city, name of province, Cuba.

Since one may not legally send dollars to Cuba and it is a great detriment for them to receive any money through the mail, the researcher may offer to make a contribution to their local church or to someone the parish priest may designate outside of Cuba.

In most instances, a reply may be expected in about six months, sometimes more, after one has mailed the letter. After a period of about 8 or 9 months, one may assume that their letter or the reply has been lost or destroyed. The author has experienced a success rate of about 60-70% using this system during the past 25 years.

The "magnus opus" about the Catholic Church in Cuba is Father Ismael Teste's _Historia Eclesiastica de Cuba._ This five volume work not only provides a brief history of all the parishes in Cuba, but it also gives a small biography for each parish priest which has served each parish.

The parishes of La Habana "intramuros" or inside the old city walls have had basically the same boundaries since 1691. These are as follow:

Cathedral Parish - bounded by "calles" Muralla, Habana, Empedrado and the waterfront.
Santo Angel - bounded by Empedrado, Monserrate and the waterfront.
Santo Cristo - bounded by Sol, Habana, Empedrado & Monserrate.
Espiritu Santo - Sol, the "calle" Habana block between Sol & Muralla, Muralla, Egido and the waterfront.

One should not neglect the Archdiocesan and Diocesan archives. This is especially true of the Archdioceses of Santiago de Cuba and La Habana. At their archives, many different types of documents from the early years may be found.

In the Archdiocesan Archive of La Habana, for example, the second section contains the files on recognition and legitimization of bastard children, amended baptismal records, files for dispensations for relatives wanting to marry and much more.

Undoubtedly, the best guide to the Archdiocesan Archive of La Habana is the work by M.Cuadrado Melo titled, Obispado de La Habana. Su Historia. This multivolume work, besides being historical, gives a listing by parish and its extant records. Its value is beyond question, especially if one realizes that these parish records are not duplicated anywhere in the world.

The baptismal, marriage and death registers were kept in various forms. Usually, there was one for white people, another known as the "general" register, was for "free" people of color. A third one was kept for slaves. The "general" registers were also used for those born out of wedlock.

If one married at the same parish where one had been baptized, then, usually, there was a marginal note placed on the baptismal record giving the date of the marriage and to whom.

If the term "exposito" is encountered, the researcher should be aware that it refers to one who was abandoned as a foundling. This Latin term literally means "out of place". Since the abandoned child's surname was not known, "exposito" itself became their surname.

Published Catholic Church Records

The early baptismal and marriage records of the Cathedral of La Habana were published in 1974 by Dr.Ferdinand Stibi. His publication titled, El "Libro de Barajas" de la Catedral de la Habana, covers marriage records from 16 July 1584 to 4 August 1622 and baptismal records from 20 January 1590 to 16 January 1600. The book is published in index form and provides the volume and number of the entry.

Through their Family History Library's microfilming program, the Church of Jesus Christ of Latter-Day Saints has also published similar Cuban re-

cords. They have microfilmed a small portion of the
extracts made by the Conde de Jaruco and his colleagues of some of the baptismal,marriage and death
registers of the Cathedral of La Habana. Though
certainly not a complete extraction, it provides a
few records which would otherwise have not come to
light. The extracts are for certain surnames only
and cover the following time periods:

Baptisms 1705-1800 Marriages 1622-1874 Deaths 1619-
1868

At the Family History Library, one may also find a
microfilm containing some Camaguey marriages from
1753 to 1780.

The Cuban Genealogical Society has published
in its Revista abstractions of the extractions of
Conde de Jaruco. These have been mainly for parishes throughout Cuba. They are arranged in a chrono-
logical manner with type of event noted. Also, the
reference number to the original abstractions.

In the Revista de la Biblioteca Nacional de
Cuba, Rafael Nieto Cortadellas published actual records of baptisms, marriages and deaths of many no-
table Cubans. Almost every issue from that of Oct-
ober-December 1953 to January-March 1957 contains
over 10 pages of records for many different individuals. Some of these are not the usual "notables"
one would expect.

Cuban Parishes in 1938

"Santiago de Cuba Province"

City/Town	Church Name	Founded
Santiago de Cuba	La Asuncion de Ntra. Sra.(Cathedral)	1514
" " "	Ntra.Sra.de Dolores transferred to	1722
" " "	Santa Lucia	1908
" " "	Santisima Trinidad	1787
" " "	Santo Tomas Apostol	1719
Banes	Ntra.Sra.de la Caridad	1909
Baracoa	Ntra.Sra.de la Asuncion	1514
Bayamo	San Salvador	1514
El Cobre	Ntra.Sra.de la Caridad	n/a

Fray Benito	Santa Florentina	n/a
Gibara	San Fulgencio	1816
Guantanamo	Santa Catalina de Ricci	1836
Jigüani	San Pablo Apostol	1700
Baire	San Bartolome	1821
Santa Rita	Santa Rita de Casia	1805
Los Negros	San Marcelino	1856
Babiney	Santa Barbara	1854
Holguin	San Isidro	1523
"	San Jose	n/a
Manzanillo	La Purisima Concepcion	1784
Mayari	San Gregorio	1557
Niquero	San Francisco Javier	1825
Palma Soriano	Ntra.Sra.del Rosario	1775
Puerto Padre	San Jose (prior San Agustin burnt 1881)	1881
Sagua de Tanamo	Santisima Trinidad	1794
San Andres (Guabasiabo)	San Andres	1756
San Luis de Los Caneyes	San Luis	1658
Victoria de las	San Jeronimo	1610

"Camagüey Province"

Camagüey	Sagrario de la Catedral	1514
"	Ntra.Sra.de la Caridad	1734
"	Ntra.Sra.de la Soledad	1697
"	Santa Ana	1550
"	Santo Cristo	1723
"	Ntra.Sra.del Carmen	1732
"	San Jose	1806
Ciego de Avila	San Eugenio de la Palma	1610
Esmeralda	San Miguel de Cubitas	1864
Florida	Ntra.Sra.del Carmen	1802
Guaimaro	La Purisima Concepcion	1799
Sibanicu	San Antonio de Padua	1799
Jatibonico	San Jose (de Arroyo Blanco)	late 18th C.
Moron	Ntra.Sra.de la Candelaria	1750
Nuevitas	Ntra.Sra.de la Caridad	1828
Santa Cruz del Sur	La Santa Cruz	1826

"Las Villas Province"

Cienfuegos	La Purisima Concepcion	1820
"	El Patrocinio de la Santisima Virgen	1904
Abreus	Ntra.Sra.del Rosario	1870

```
Aguada de Pasajeros   Jesus Nazareno           1938
Alvarez               San Narciso              1688
Caibarien             La Purisima Concepcion   1841
Camajuani             San Jose                 1880
Cartagena (Rodas)     Ntra.Sra.de la Caridad   1859
Ceja de Pablo         San Pedro y San Pablo    1688
  (Corralillo)
Cifuentes             Santa Maria Magdalena    1817
Cruces                La Invencion de la Cruz  1876
Cumanayagua           San Felipe y La Santa    1743
                        Cruz
Encrucijada(El Santo)San Francisco de Paula    1862
Esperanza             Ntra.Sra.de la Esperanza 1809
Fomento (Sipiado)     Ntra.Sra.del Rosario      n/a
Jibaro                San Antonio Abad         1816
Banao                 San Ignacio de Loyola    1862
Palmira               Ntra.Sra.del Rosario     1842
Placetas              San Atanasio             1684
Quemados de Güines    La Purisima Concepcion   1667
Sagua la Grande       La Purisima Concepcion   1859
San Antonio de las    Ntra.Sra.de los Angeles  1858
  Vueltas
San Fernando          Ntra.Sra.de la Cande-    1743
  de Camarones          laria
San Juan de los       La Santa Cruz y San      1515
  Remedios              Bautista
Santa Clara           La Divina Pastora        1689
  "       "           Ntra.Sra.de la Cande-    1724
                        laria
Santa Isabel de las   San Antonio de Padua     1820
  Lajas
Sancti Spiritus       Espiritu Santo           1514
  "       "           Ntra.Sra.de la Caridad   1727
Santo Domingo         Ntra.Sra.de los Dolores  1819
Trinidad              Santisima Trinidad       1514
  "                   Ntra.Sra.de la Cande-    late
                        laria (La Popa)        17th C.
  "                   Santa Ana                1800
Yaguajay              San Antonio de Padua     1857
                        (prior San Jose)

          "Province of Matanzas"

Matanzas              San Carlos Borromeo      1693
                        (Cathedral)
Pueblo Nuevo          San Juan Bautista        1832
Versalles             San Pedro Apostol        1870
Rio y Capricho        Ntra.Sra.de la Caridad   1936
La Playa              La Virgen Milagrosa      1955
Agramonte (Cuevitas)  Ntra.Sra.de la Paz       1879

                        23
```

Alacranes	San Francisco de Paula	1688
Amarillas	Sagrado Corazon de Jesus	1890
Arabos (Palmillas)	La Purisima Concepcion	1688
Arcos de Canasi	San Matias Apostol	1738
Bolondron	La Purisima Concepcion	1808
San Antonio de Cabezas	San Antonio de Padua	1822
Camarioca	Ntra.Sra.de la Caridad	1817
Cardenas (Guamacaro)	La Purisima Concepcion	1840
Canasi	San Matias Apostol	1813
Carlos Rojas (Cimarrones)	Ntra.Sra.de la Caridad	1819
Ceiba Mocha	San Agustin y Ntra.Sra. de la Candelaria	1797
Colon	San Jose	1836
Cidra	Santa Ana (burnt 1935)	1813
Corral Nuevo	Ntra.Sra.del Rosario	1812
Jagüey Grande	Ntra.Sra.de Altagracia	1688
Corral Falso (Macuriges)	Santa Catalina Martir	1661
Jovellanos (Bemba)	Ntra.Sra.de la Asuncion	1863
Mendez Capote (Lagunillas)	San Juan Bautista	1821
Limonar (Guamacaro)	La Purisima Concepcion y San Cipriano	1688
Marti (Hato Nuevo)	San Jose y San Hilario	1688
Maximo Gomez (Recreo)	San Francisco Javier	1835
Perico (EL Roque)	San Miguel y Santa Catalina de Sena	1838
Sabanilla del Encomendador	La Santa Cruz	1747
San Jose de los Ramos	San Jose(burnt in 1911)	1572
Union de Reyes	Ntra.Sra.de la Caridad (burnt in 1933)	1876
Varadero	Inmaculado Caorazon de Maria	1880

"Province of La Habana"

La Habana	San Cristobal (Cathedral)	1519
"	Espiritu Santo	1638
"	Santo Cristo	1640
"	Santo Angel Custodio	1690
"	Jesus, Maria y Jose	1753
"	Ntra.Sra.de Monserrate	1675

La Habana	Ntra.Sra.de la Caridad	1739
	(originally Guadalupe)	
"	Ntra.Sra.del Pilar	1816
"	San Nicolas de Bari	1854
"	Ntra.Sra.del Carmen	1666
Jesus del Monte	El Buen Pastor	1698
Cerro	El Salvador del Mundo	1800
Arroyo Apolo	San Francisco de Paula	1665
Vedado	El Sagrado Corazon de Jesus	1879
Aguacate	San Lorenzo (prior Ntra. Sra.del Carmen)	1756
Alquizar	San Agustin	1779
Batabano	San Pedro Apostol y La Divina Pastora	1668
Bauta(Hoyo Colorado)	Ntra.Sra.de las Mercedes	1688
Bejucal	San Felipe y Santiago	1722
Caimito del Guayabal	San Francisco de Asis	1865
Calabazar	San Juan Bautista y San Antonio de Padua	1861
Campo Florido	Santa Ana de Guanabo	1803
Bacuranao	Ntra.Sra.de los Dolores	1668
Peñalver(Guanabacoa)	San Jeronimo y Ntra. Sra.de los Dolores	1783
Caraballo	San Pablo	1803
Casa Blanca	Ntra.Sra.del Carmen	1790
Casiguas	San Pedro Apostol	1790
Catalina de Güines	Santa Catalina Martir	1670
Ceiba del Agua	San Luis Gonzaga y Santo Cristo	1763
El Calvario	La Invencion de la Santa Cruz	1735
El Cano	La Purisima Concepcion	1688
Guanabacoa	Ntra.Sra.de la Asuncion	1576
Guara	Santisima Trinidad	1688
Guatao	Ntra.Sra.del Rosario	1750
Güira de Melena	San Jose	1779
Isla de Pinos	Ntra.Sra.de lo Dolores y San Nicolas	1627
Jaruco	San Juan Bautista & Inmaculada Concepcion	1778
La Salud	Santo Cristo de la Salud	1802
La Sierra(Marianao)	San Agustin	1930
Los Quemados de Marianao	San Francisco Javier	1734
Madruga	Ntra.Sra.de Regla y San Luis	1688
Nueva Paz	Ntra.Sra.de la Paz	1688
Managua	San Isidro Labrador	1730
Pipian	Ntra.Sra.del Rosario	1794

Puentes Grandes	San Jeronimo	1817
Quivican	San Pedro Apostol	1667
Regla	Ntra.Sra.de Regla	1690
San Antonio de los Baños	San Antonio Abad	1784
San Antonio del Rio Blanco	San Antonio de Padua	1783
San Antonio de las Vegas	San Antonio de Padua	1712
San Jose de las Lajas	San Jose	1778
San Julian de Güines	San Julian	1688
San Matias de Rio Blanco	San Matias	1768
San Miguel del Padron	San Miguel Arcangel	1668
San Nicolas	San Nicolas de Bari	1823
Santa Maria del Rosario	Ntra.Sra.del Rosario	1732
Santiago de las Vegas	Santiago El Mayor	1688
Tapaste	La Purisima Concepcion	1785
Vereda Nueva	Ntra.Sra.del Pilar	1802
Wajay	Ntra.Sra.de la Candelaria	1764

"Province of Pinar del Rio"

Pinar del Rio	San Rosendo (Cathedral)	1571
Alonso Rojas	Ntra.Sra.de Guadalupe	1857
Artemisa	San Marcos	1805
Bahia Honda	San Jose	1794
Baja (Dimas)	La Visitacion de Santa Isabel	1767
Cabañas(La Dominica)	Ntra.Sra.de Guadalupe	1823
Candelaria	Ntra.Sra.de la Candelaria	1811
Cayajabos	San Francisco Xavier	1798
Consolacion del Norte	Ntra.Sra.del Rosario	1569
Consolacion del Sur	Ntra.Sra.de la Candelaria	1690
Las Mangas	San Juan Nepomuceno	1789
Las Pozas (Cacarajicara)	San Basilio el Magno	1675
Los Palacios	Jesus Nazareno	1760
Mantua	Ntra.Sra.de las Nieves	1750
Mariel	Santa Teresa de Jesus	1804
Puerta de la Güira	Ntra.Sra.del Carmen	1806

Quiebra Hacha	Ntra.Sra.de las Mercedes	1800
San Diego de los Banos	San Diego	1851
San Diego de Nuñez	Ntra.Sra.del Carmen	1805
San Luis de los Pinos	San Joaquin	1829
San Juan y Martinez	San Juan Bautista	1761
San Cayetano	La Purisima Concepcion	1840
San Cristobal	El Nino de Jesus de Los Pinos y La Santa Cruz	1688

Non-Catholic Church Records

Protestant and Jewish religious denominations did not begin to make inroads in Cuba until well into the 19th century. Even so, it was not until the coming of independence from Spain and the United States that non-Catholic churches became widethroughout the island. With the secularization of previously Catholic institutions, such as marriage, a clear separation between church and state became evident.

At the turn of the 19th century into the 20th, the beginnings of what would become a sizable Jewish community began to arrive in Cuba. The United Hebrew Congregation was formed in La Habana in 1904. Its first cemetery was opened in Guanabacoa in 1906.

The restrictive American immigration policy in the wake of the First World War, diverted a great many Jewish immigrants to Cuba which would have otherwise settled in the United States.

In 1914, the Shevet Ahim congregation had been formed in La Habana. About 1916, the "Asociacion de Jovenes Hebreos" was founded and set up offices at calle Obispo 97.

In 1924, the Jewish Committee for Cuba was begun in New York as an aid society to all the Jews in Cuba. One of its aims was also to bring together under one representative banner the various Jewish communities in Cuba. With the advent of the Second World War in Europe, a Joint Relief Committee was set up in La Habana in order to aid the many refugees trying to escape from the war.

The end of the war brought a decline in the Jewish population of Cuba, although in 1959 there were still five temples in La Habana. These were in founding order: United Hebrew Congregation, Patronato, Adath Israel, Union Hebrea and El Centro.

Various publications were published at various times by some of the Jewish congregations. The primary ones were Havaner Lebn Almanach from 1933 to 1948, Oifgang from July 1927 to September 1930, El Estudiante Hebreo from 1928 to 1931 and a few other minor publications. Except for those which the extant congregations may possess, the marriage, death and circumcision files of past congregations have not been located.Equally so,for the immigration files begun after 1933 by the Joint Relief Committee.

In 1874,the following Protestant churches were located in La Habana:

Episcopal Church, Central Chapel,located within the Pasaje Hotel on the Prado.
Baptist Church—Gethsemani on the corner of Dragones and Zulueta streets.
Methodist Church, Central Chapel Jerusalem, located at calle Concordia 81.

In the present day there is a Methodist Church in the Vedado section of La Habana which was founded in 1883. Their address is as follows: Iglesia Metodista del Vedado "Rev.Miguel Soto Asensi",calle K #502, esq.25, Vedado, C.Habana 4, Cuba 10400.

There are some extant marriage and baptismal records from the British Consulate in La Habana. There are 22 marriages which occurred between October 1842 and November 1849 while there are two baptismal records each for the years 1847 and 1848. These are available from the Public Record Office in London, England under their reference Spain RG-33/155.

It should be noted that the most popular of the Catholic churches for the English—speaking worshippers was the Santo Cristo Church because they offered one Sunday service in English. It is wise also to note the locations of the various consulates at different times, since various nationalities had a tendency to congregate their dwellings around or near their country's consulate.

Churches of all denominations and sects have all endured the same persecution and restrictions under the CASTRO regime.

Religious References

Dominguez Rodriguez, Mons.Jose M. Notas Cronologicas Sobre las Parroquias de la Diocesis de Matanzas. La Habana, 1963.

Urrutia Montoya, Dr. Ignacio J. de. Los Tres Primeros Historiadores de la Isla de Cuba. Imp. Andres Pego, La Habana, 1876, 3 vols.

Fernandez Escobio, Fernando. El obispo Compostela y la Iglesia Cubana del siglo XVII.

------Raices Cubanas, Iglesias y Camposantos Coloniales. Miami, 1991.

Gonzalez Davila, Gil. Teatro Eclesiastico de la Primitiva Iglesia de las Indias Occidentales. 1649, 2 vols.

Lopetegui, L. Historia de la Iglesia en la America Española. 1965.

Koehler, Max S. "Los Judios en Cuba", Revista Bimestre Cubana. July-August, 1920.

Cantor, Aviva. "Being Jewish within the Revolution" Cuba Review, vol. 9, no.1, 1979, 25-31.

Leroy, Luis Felipe & Mons. A. Gaztelu. Fray Geronimo Valdes, obispo de Cuba. La Iglesia Parroquial del Espiritu Santo de La Habana. La Habana, 1963.

Sapir, Boris. The Jewish Community of Cuba. 1948.

Nieman, Genia. "The Jews of Cuba", Doña Genia, April, 1979.

Romero Gutierrez, Maria L. La Iglesia en Cuba en el Siglo XVII. Sevilla, Spain 1972.

Geiger, Maynard J. "Biographical Dictionary of the Franciscans in Spanish Florida and Cuba, 1528 to 1841", in Franciscan Studies, v. 21, 1940.

LeBroc, Reinero. *Cuba, Iglesia y Sociedad.* Madrid, 1976.

Chaurrondo, Hilario. *Los PP.Paules en las Antillas.* La Habana, 1925.

Morell de Santa Cruz, Pedro Agustin. *Historia de la Isla y Catedral de Cuba.* Academia de la Historia de Cuba, 1929.

Garcia de Arboleya, Jose. *Manuel de la Isla de Cuba, compendio de su historia, geografia, estadistica y administracion.* La Habana, 1852.

CIVIL REGISTRATION

By Royal Decree of 8 January and 8 November 1884, the Spanish law of civil registration of 1870 was applied to Cuba and Puerto Rico. So, in effect, it was not until 1885 when civil registration began in Cuba. However, it would not be until 1889 that a specific civil marriage law would be passed.

It took Cuba's independence from Spain to bring about a more drastic change and widespread compliance. From April and August, 1899 until 31 December 1900, a grace period was granted to those whose births or marriages had not been properly registered up to that time.

Additionally, by order dated 5 September 1900, parish priests were to receive 10 cents for every death certificate they issued at the request of a municipal judge. The filing of a civil marriage certificate, whether the ceremony was civil or religious, was made compulsory in Agust of 1900.

However, the church and state were not officially separated until 1901. It took until 1918 to make a civil marriage compulsory even if a religious one had already taken place.

If one was in Cuba, it would only be a matter of going to the "Juzgado Municipal" (municipal judge) of the district where the person was registered to request whatever record one wanted. The wait would be very long, but sooner or later, one obtain the document.

However, outside of Cuba,the procedure becomes costly, lengthy and with no guarantees that a record will be found or provided. This is true even in the countries which have diplomatic relations with Cuba. Still if a researcher wants to pursue this route, then they should check with the Cuban Consulate or Embassy in their respective country of residence for further details.

Many different publications mention vital statistics. These are not always limited to famous people, so when reading or thumbing through any publication, one should make a note of these for future reference, (see also NEWSPAPER RECORDS).

La Habana "Juzgados Municipales" in 1919

In 1919, there were six "Juzgados Municipales" in La Habana. Their boundaries covered the following "barrios":

Juzgado Municipal del Norte (north) - Santo Angel, Punta, Colon, Monserrate, San Leopoldo, Dragones and Guadalupe.

Juzgado Municipal del Sur (south) - Tacon, Marte, Penalver, San Nicolas, Ceiba, Vives, Jesus Maria and Arsenal.

Juzgado Municipal del Este (east) - San Juan de Dios, Templete, San Francisco, Paula, Santo Cristo, San Felipe, Santa Teresa, Santa Clara, San Isidro and the bay.

Juzgado Municipal del Oeste (west) - Chavez, Pueblo Nuevo, Villanueva and Cerro.

Juzgado Municipal del Centro (central) - Pilar, Atares, Manuel de la Cruz, Jesus del Monte and Luyano.

Juzgado Municipal del Vedado - Vedado, Medina, Principe, San Lazaro and Cayo Hueso.

For the boundaries of the "barrios" in 1900 see pages 92 to 94.

NOTARIAL RECORDS

Notarial records are of prime importance in the lives of Spanish as well as other European people. It was natural then, that being a Spanish colony, uba would adopt the Spanish system.

Everything, or almost everything, in the life of a person was recorded in a notarial records. A few of these records include, but are not limited to business contracts, marriage contracts, land exchanges, wills, powers of attorney and many others. The "escribano" or notary would have registered and kep copies of these in his "protocolo" or registry.

There were two main types of "escribanos". One was the "escribano real" or royal notary and the other was the "escribano publico" or public notary. For La Habana, these records are housed at the Archivo de Protocolos within the Archivo Nacional de Cuba (ANC). For the early period of Cuban history, the records of other towns or cities on the island may be found here. For later periods, one needs to consult the municipal or provincial archives.

One did not have to be rich and powerful to make use of the notaries or "escribanias". There are many instances where illeterate citizens used them to give power of attorney to an educated individual who was capable of handling their affairs or lived in the particular locality where a business deal would take place.

In volumes 8 to 11 of the <u>Boletin del Archivo Nacional de Cuba</u>, an index was published. This is by no means a surname index. This is an index by notary and year which tells what type of record is available for that particular notary and year. The records are for the years of 1842 to 1890.

In volume 24 of the <u>Publicaciones del Archivo Nacional de Cuba</u>, on page 253 of the article titled "Historia de los Archivos de Cuba" by Joaquin Llaverias, there is a listing of the various notaries, their extant records and number of volumes. The notaries were usually known by an official name or by the name of the person who had been the first notary at that location.

33

On 12 April 1898, the Register of Last Wills was established so that records of wills would be kept separate from other notarial documents. These records would be found among those of the municipal governments.

Other cities with large notarial collections are Santa Clara with its collection dating from 1690, Santiago de Cuba from 1730 and Trinidad from 1740.

Notarial References

Rojas, Maria Teresa de. Indice y Extractos del Archivo de Protocolos de la Habana. Imp. Ucar, Garcia y Cia., La Habana, 1947-57.
vol.1-Juan Perez de Borroto notary 1578-9,82.
Martin Calvo de la Puerta 1584-5.
vol.2- "   "   "   "   "   1586-7.
vol.3- "   "   "   "   "   1588.
vol.4- "   "   "   "   "   1589-91.

Garcia del Pino, Cesar & Alicia Melis Cappa. El Libro de los Escribanos Cubanos de los Siglos XVI, XVII, XVIII. Editorial de Ciencias Sociales, La Habana, 1982.

"Catalogo de los Fondos Americanos del Archivo de Protocolos de Sevilla", in Coleccion de Documentos Ineditos para la Historia de Hispanoamerica. 1930-2, volumes x,xi,xiv.

Academia de la Historia de Cuba. Papeles Existentes en el Archivo General de Indias para la Historia de Cuba. Imp.El Siglo XX, Lq Habana, 1931, Publicaciones vol.2.

LAND RECORDS

Beginning in 1536, the Cabildo of Sancti Spiritus began the practice of distributing all Royal Lands (realengos) without having to receive confirmation from the Crown. The first land grant or "merced" had been made by Governor VELAZQUEZ in 1516. However, his grants and those following until 1536 had to be confirmed by the Crown.

The "merced" system granted the land to individuals which held title in usufruct, but did not own the land. It lasted until 1729.

There were three different types of grants:

1) Hatos — to be used for cattle raising, horses and mules.
2) Corrales — to be used for raising hogs.
3) Estancias — to be used for farming. These were usually the closest to the towns.

As an example of a "merced" one can check the records of the "cabildos" which are both the town meetings or the council itself. In the "Cabildo de La Habana" held on 24 January 1566, Melchor RODRIGUEZ petitioned the council that a "merced" of a savannah at Hanabana be granted to him so that he could build a cow pasture for the benefit of this city and for the vessels which pass through her port.

The "regidores" or aldermen made the grant. Many other records of this type may be found in the publication, Actas Capitulares del Ayuntamiento de La Habana. Additionally, the "protocolo" records are filled with these land records.

A good guide to "realengos" is Rodrigo de Bernardo Estrada's work titled, Prontuario de mercedes, o sea, indice por order alfabetico de las mercedes concedidas por el excmo.ayuntamiento de La Habana. It was published in 1857. Its main drawback is that it does not include minor grants.

The ANC has records of "realengos" from 1682 to 1850 in its holdings. An index by name of property and/or person was published in the Boletin volumes VIII to XII.

Just as records of "mercedes" for other cities and towns in Cuba may be found in their "cabildo" records, other land-related records may also be located at the "ayuntamientos" or city halls. Mortgage papers or "hipotecas and records from the "Registro de la Propiedad" (Property Registry or Recorder) are very useful for later property transactions outside of royal lands.

References

Noda, Tranquilino Sandalio de. "Hatos y Corrales de la Isla de Cuba", Revista de Maestros de Obras y Agrimensores. La Habana, 1890.

Ruiz Cadalso, A. & A. Segura Cabrera. Mercedes y Centros de Haciendas Circulares Cubanas. Imp. El Siglo XX, La Habana, 1916.

LeRiverend, Julio. "Vecindades y Estancias", Islas II, Santa Clara, 1960.

Corbitt, Duvon C. "Mercedes y Realengos: A Survey of the Public Land System in Cuba" in Hispanic American Historical Review, vol. XIX, (1939), 262-285.

CENSUS RECORDS

Throughout the history of Cuba, there have been many censuses, "padrones" and "matriculas" of the population. These have been of a local or national character and taken by the civil or ecclesiastical authorities.

Before continuing with the recapitulation of the censuses, it is necessary to interject and explanation of the Spanish terms "censo", "padron" and "matricula".

"Censo" may refer to a census of population, housing or business. However, the term may also mean or refer to the payment of a pension, rent or even a poll-tax.

"Padron" is a register or list of taxpayers in a particular location. The Catholic Church also took "padrones" of its resident members. On the other hand, "matricula" is a register or list of anything and not just people.

Following is a list of official island-wide population censuses made during colonial times:

1774 – Although the first official census with a modern scope was not made until 1827, there were several done prior to this which are of significance. The 1774 census was the first of these. It was ordered by Marques DE LA TORRE. The possibility exists that it was actually taken in 1775. The population it counted was 172,000.

1791 – This census was ordered by Governor Luis DE LAS CASAS. This census may have been taken in 1792. The population was 272,141.

1817 – This census was ordered by Governor CIENFUE-GOS and showed that the population had risen to 572,363.

1827 – This was the first modern official census of Cuba. The information gathered was classied by departments and other jurisdictions. The scope included the names of the inhabitants, sex, age, race and martital status.

1841 – The second modern census of Cuba. The scope was very similar to the census of 1827.

1861 – The third modern census of Cuba was taken on 14 March 1861 by the Junta General de Estadistica. It is similar in scope to the 1841 census, but also includes the civil status (whether free or slave), occupation, literacy, nationality, residence and infirmities. Apparently, a recount was done in 1862 as this census sometimes is found in the literature as the 1861-2 census.

1877 – This census was taken on 31 December 1877 by the Direccion eneral del Instituto Geografico y Estadistico. The scope included the names of the inhabitants, nationality, race and sex.

1887 – This was the final census of Cuba taken by the Spanish authorities. It was similar in scope to that of 1877. These last two censuses were taken in conjunction with those on the Spanish peninsula.

It is difficult to ascertain the location of the original schedules for the censuses taken by the Spanish authorities. The records for those of 1774, 1791 and 1817 have disappeared since they are not in the AGI, AHN or ANC.

The records for the censuses of 1827, 1841 and 1861 may be located at the Biblioteca Nacional de Cuba(BNC) in La Habana. The records for those of 1877 and 1887 also have been lost as they are not in any archive in Spain nor Cuba. The originals of the 1861 census for the northern district of Matanzas are in its Museo Municipal.

One of the extant church "padrones" of San Luis, Pinar del Rio for 1848 was published in Luis O. Escobar's book Ensayo Historico de San Luis de Occidente published in Miami in 1980. An index of this census was published in the July 1991 issue of the Revista of the Cuban Genealogical Society by the author.

Various other ecclesiastic "padrones" might be in existence within the records of the Catholic archives throughout the island or at the parishes.

Censuses under the American Administration

Two population and agricultural censuses were taken under American administration, one in 1899 and the other in 1907. Statistical volumes were published in both cases. The one for 1899 contains a list of enumerators by district as its Appendix XIII. These people were hired locally so that these lists provide a clue to their places of residence.

Sadly, the original schedules for both of them were ordered destroyed by an Act of Congress in 1910. Sometime later, the actual destruction took place.

In addition, a census of school-age children between the ages of 6 and 18 was ordered by the Military Government and conducted by the Board of Education. This census gives not only the name, age, sex, color, and place of residence for each child, but also the name of the parent supplying the information. Some of these are still preserved in the ANC and municipal archives.

Censuses under the Republic of Cuba

1919 – This census was conducted by the Direccion General del Censo. The scope included name, number of inhabitants within the household, age, sex, illegitimate children, places of residence, race, occupation, citizenship, place of birth, marital status and a few other minor categories. The electoral census was taken simultaneously, (see OFFICIAL RECORDS). A report was printed both in Spanish and English.

1931 – Its scope was similar to that of 1919 and it was also conducted by the Direccion General del Censo. A somewhat final report was published in 1978.

1943 – Again both the population and electoral censuses were conducted simultaneously by the Direccion General del Censo. Similar in scope to previous ones, this time the places of birth of the parents and the person's year of arrival in Cuba, if foreign born, were included.

1953 – Similar in scope to previous censuses, this one was taken by the Oficina Nacional de los Censos Demograficos y Electoral. This census was conducted according to the 1950 Census of the Americas (COTA) program. A one volume report was published in Spanish. It was conducted at the same time as housing and electoral censuses.

1970 – This census counted the population as of the 6th of September and was conducted by the Direccion Central de Estadistica. The United States" Naval Base at Guantanamo was not included as in previous ones. Its scope was typical of other censuses. So far, three volumes of statistics have been published.

1981 – By the time of this census, Cuba had been divided into 13 provinces instead of the previous six. Its scope was based on recommendations made by the United Nations and is typical of modern censuses.

1987 – This census was taken as of 31 December 1987 at which time the population was deemed to be 10,356,442.

These and other statistics are kept by the Direccion Central de Estadistica. The national repository is the Centro de Informacion Cientifico-tecnica, Comite Estatal de Estadistica, C. Habana, Cuba.

Miscellaneous Census Records

Beginning in October of 1812, the "Comisarios de la Policia" (police commissaries) kept biennial "padrones" related to the issuance of the "cedulas personales" (personal identification cards) which were issued by local neighborhood mayors. In every city or town of any consequence, these were required.

These "cedulas" had the person's name, place of birth (city and province), age, marital status, profession and physical description. Parents were responsible for obtaining them for their children as well until the age of majority was reached. Although normally there was a charge, poor people obtained them for free. This system lasted until 1878.

In 1947, a Primer Censo de la Industria Tabacalera was taken and published. This census of tobacco-workers gives the name of the employer as well as their location.

Three additional sources for non-population censuses were published. One is the Censo Agricola taken by the provincial Matanzas government in 1881 and published in 1883. It concerns sugar plantations and their workers.

The Ministerio de Agricultura published the other two non-population census sources. These are the Memoria del Censo Agricola Nacional published in 1946 and the Memoria del Censo Ganadero published in 1952. The first concerns agriculture and the second cattle ranching. They are for available at National Library of Agriculture in Washington, D.C.

Census References

Ortiz Fernandez, Fernando. "Cuadro de los Pricipales Censos de la Poblacion de Cuba desde 1532 a 1907", in Hampa Afro-Cubana: Los Negros Esclavos: Estudio Sociologico y de Derecho Publico. La Habana, 1916.

Estado General de la Poblacion de la Isla de Cuba, dispuesto por el Excmo. Sr. Jose Cienfuegos y acuerdo para que sirviera de base a las elecciones de 1821. Imp. del Gobierno, La Habana, 1821.

Comision de Estadistica. Cuadro estadistico de la siempre fiel isla de Cuba correspondiente al año 1827..., La Habana, 1829.

Censo de la siempre fidelisima ciudad de La Habana, 1828. Imp.del Gobierno, La Habana, 1829.

Resumen del Censo de Poblacion de la Isla de Cuba a Fin del Año 1841. Imp.del Gobierno, La Habana, 1842.

Comision de Estadistica. Cuadro estadistico de la siempre fiel Isla de Cuba,1846.La Habana,1847.

Junta General de Estadistica. Anuario Estadistico
de la Espana...1857. Madrid, 1859.

Junta General de Estadistica. Censo de la Poblacion de Espana segun el recuento verificado en
25 de diciembre de 1860. Madrid, 1863.

Armildez de Toledo, Conde. Noticias estadisticas
de la Isla de Cuba en 1861, dispuestas y pu-
blicadas por el Centro de Estadisticas. La Habana, 1864.

"Resumen General del Censo de Poblacion de la Isla
de Cuba en 31 de diciembre de 1877" in Boletin
Oficial del Ministerio de Ultramar, 1879. Madrid, 1889?

"El Censo Cubano de 1877 y sus diferentes versio-
nes" in Santiago (34):167-216, June 1979.

Intendencia General de Hacienda. Poblacion, estudios estadistico-demograficos correspondientes
a 1879. La Habana, 1881.

Provincia de Matanzas, Seccion de Fomento y Estadisticas. Censo de Poblacion en 1880. Imp.
Aurora del Yumuri, Matanzas, 1881.

Junta General de Estadistica. Censo de la Poblacion de España segun el empadronamiento hecho
en 31 de diciembre de 1887. Madrid, 1889.

War Department, Office of the Director of Census of
Cuba. Report on the Census of Cuba, 1899.
Government Printing Office, Washington, D.C.,
1900.

Oficina Nacional del Censo. Censo de la Republica
de Cuba bajo la administracion provisional de
los Estados Unidos, 1907. Washington, D.C.,
1908.

Direccion General del Censo. Censo de la Republica
de Cuba, 1919. Maza, Arroyo y Caso, La Habana,
1919.

Oficina Nacional de los Censos Demografico y Electoral. Censo de Poblacion, Vivienda y Electoral, 1953. La Habana, 1955.

Perez de la Riva, Juan. "Estudios y Estadísticas Demograficas" in Revista de la Biblioteca Nacional "Jose Marti". Ano 58, no. 1, 1967.

Bourde, Guy. "Fuentes y metodos de la historia demografica en Cuba (siglos XVIII y XIX)" in Revista de la Biblioteca Nacional "Jose Marti". no. 1, 1974.

Konetzke, Richard (ed.). Coleccion de documentos para la historia de la formacion social de Hispanoamerica, 1493-1810. Madrid, 1953-62, 3 vols.

Sanchez Albornoz, N. & J.L. Moreno. La Poblacion de America Latina; bosquejo historico. Buenos Aires, 1968.

Centro de Estudios Demograficos. La Poblacion de Cuba. Editorial de Ciencias Sociales, La Habana, 1976.

OFFICIAL PASSENGER RECORDS

Official records of passenger departures from Spain are housed in the AGI. These are of incalculable value because they may lead one to the place of origin of the immigrant.

In section III of the AGI titled, "Casa de la Contratacion", the records regarding passengers are classified. This early colonial government agency was responsible for all the commerce and travel between Spain and her colonies from 1509 to 1790.

They kept "Libros de asientos de pasajeros a Indias, 1509 to 1701". These records are contained within legajos 5536- 5540. These passenger books record the names of the emigrants as well as their places of residence or birthplace. The only legal port of departure from Spain from 1509 to 1701 was Sevilla (Seville).

Another AGI subsection titled, "Informaciones y licensias de pasajeros" covers the period from 1534 to 1790 and contains copies of petitions for travel to the colonies to conduct all manner of business. These records are filed within legajos 5217-5535.

An additional source of emigrant records may be located in the section, "Contaduria" in legajos 240-244. These are records of licenses to travel to the Indies, "Licensias para pasar a Indias, 1556-1671.

An index has been in preparation for the two subsections under "Contratacion". So far, five volumes have been published covering the period from 1509 to 1577: <u>Catalogo de Pasajeros a Indias durantelos siglos XVI, XVII, XVIII, redactado por el personal facultativo del Archivo General de Indias.</u> Volume 1 covers the period from 1509 to 1534, volume 2-1535 to 1538, volume 3-1539 to 1559, volume 4-1560 to 1566 and volume 5-1567 to 1577.

Although no published index exists for the period from 1577 to 1790, one may write the AGI with an ancestor's name and approximate period of departure requesting that a search of the card index be made. If an entry is found, it will be sent.

For earlier records,the researcher should consult Peter Bowman's publication, Indice geobiogra-
fico de Cuarenta Mil Pobladores Espanoles de America en el Siglo XVI published in Bogota, Colombia in
1964 and a second volume in Mexico in 1968. These
cover the period from 1493 to 1539.

During the first third of the 19th century,one
may find "licensias de embarque" or embarking licenses in the "Ultramar" and "Santo Domingo" sections of the AGI. After 1835, these may be located
in the AHN. These licenses ususally give the name,
age, place of birth and may be accompanied by baptismal records.

The Directorio de Artes, Comercio e Industrias
de La Habana for 1859 makes mention that upon arrival at any Cuban port, the captain of each vessel
had to present to the authorities a list of passengers and their passports. Using these two documents
the authorities would then issue to every disembarking passenger "boletas de desembarco" or disembarking tickets. These were used as a form of identification card while on the island.

During that time, everyone needed a passport
for travel to Cuba including Spanish citizens. Additionally, foreigners had to secure a visa from
the nearest Spanish Consulate to their embarkation
point. The only exceptions were ships' crews and
and those passengers who had lost them because of a
vessel sinking.

If foreigners were going to spend three or
more months on the island, then upon arrival, they
had to secure a "carta de domicilio" which may be
said to be comparable to modern residency cards.

The petitioners would obtain a certificate of
good moral character and intentions for staying in
Cuba from their local consulate. This certificate
would then be presented to the Captain General for
review along with an application. The main qualifi-
cation, other than being of good moral character,
was that they be engaged in commerce or useful emp-
loyment. These records are found in the ANC in the
section titled, "Gobierno Superior Civil" in the
subsection "registro de extranjeros".

The Scottish Genealogist published two short

articles by F.J.R. Henderson detailing the extant "carta de domicilio" records for Scottish,Irish and English individuals. The published records covered the periods of 1818 to 1819, 1853 to 1858 and one in 1865. These may be found in volume 11, November 1964 and volume 17, June 1970 of the mentioned periodical.

The ANC has in its section called, "Aduana de La Habana" (Havana customshouse), the passenger arrival lists and disembarking tickets among all the documentation dating between 1827 to 1906. This section is supposed to have a card index by first surname.

Naturalization records of Chinese and Yucatanese from 1819 to 1869 are contained within legajos 785 to 813 of the ANC. These people migrated and were brought to Cuba as a source of cheap labor much as in the building of the western railroads in the United States. Between 1848 to 1874, more than 124,000 arrived in La Habana.

For those of Galician ancestry or "gallegos", it should be noted that heavy migration from this region did not begin until 1848. Prior to this time, other regions of Spain predominated in sending colonists to Cuba. For a thorough article on Galician migration to the New World see "La Emigracion Gallega a America" by Luisa Cuesta. This is located in the journal, Arquivos de Estudios Gallegos, volume IV, pages 141-217, published in 1932 in Santiago de Compostela, Spain.

Depending on the time period, one should not overlook the many immigrations and emigrations that Cuba has endured due to the political climate or conflicts. These upheavals have caused not only Cubans to leave the island, but some have brought non-Spanish immigrants to Cuba.

One of the first large-scale migration was the one that occurred as a result of the Spanish having ceded Florida to England in 1763 and taking it back in 1784.

The first non-Spanish nor Cuban migration, was brought about by the revolution in Haiti on the island of Hispaniola. This caused many French citizens to come to Cuba in the late 18th and early 19th

centuries. Their stay in Cuba was short-lived since
by March 1808 many were forced to leave. Though a
few returned to France, a great many of them found
their way to Mexico and the United States.

During the American Civil War, many Southern-
ers and Northerners travelled to La Habana, Matanzas, Cardenas and other major Cuban ports. Some
went to Cuba to escape the war, others went as merchants to acquire supplies for their respective
sides in the war and others as spies.

In addition, at various times, many immigrants
from other Spanish colonies went to Cuba seeking
refuge from their particular troubles and wars of
independence.

One should be aware that not every immigrant
went to the Spanish colonies legally nor by going
through the proper channels. Therefore, many will
not appear in these records simply because they did
not seek permission to travel to the New World or
to land in a certain place.

Also, many others were exempt from the various
requirements for licenses and passports. These were
usually people in prominent administrative or military positions as well as those of the nobility.

Migration References

The following publications provide information
on emigration from Spain to the colonies. Though
not all pertain to Cuba only, those that do not may
provide a lead to where records may be located. At
the end of the list, the references for some migration records are provided.

Cuba. Secretaria de Hacienda. Inmigracion y Movi-
miento de Pasajeros. Annual Publication,1907.

Rubio Moreno, Luis (ed.). "Pasajeros a Indias,1534
to 1575" in Coleccion de documentos ineditos
para la historia de Hispanoamerica. Madrid,
1930, vol. 8.

Friede, Juan. "Spanish Emigration to America to
1550" in Hispanic American Historical Review,
vol. XXXI, 1951, 331-348.

Badura, Bohumil. "Los Franceses en Santiago de Cuba a Mediados del Ano 1808" in Ibero-Americana Pragensia, V, Prague 1971, 157-160.

Boyd-Bowman, Peter. "La Emigracion Peninsular a America, 1520-1539" in Historia Mexicana, vol.13, no. 50, 1963, 37-71.

Boyd-Bowman, Peter. "La Procedencia de los Españoles de America, 1540-1559" in Historia Mexicana, vol. 17, no. 65, 1967, 37-71.

Delgado, Jaime. "Extranjeros para la America Española", in Revista de Indias, vol. VIII, no. 28 and 29, 1947, 485-496.

Bilbao, Jon. Vascos en Cuba 1492-1511. Editorial Vasca Ekin, SRL, Buenos Aires, 1918.

Steffy, Joan Marie. The Cuban mmigration of Tampa, Florida, 1886-1898. MA Thesis, University of South Florida, 1975.

Torres Lanzas, Pedro. Catalogo de Legajos del AGI. Seccion Tercera (third section). Sevilla, 1921-1922, 2 vols.

Montes, Elices. Los Asturianos en el Norte y los Asturianos en Cuba. Imp. La Universal, La Habana, 1893.

Maduell, Charles R. Index of Spanish Citizens Entering the Port of New Orleans between January 1820 to December 1839. New Orleans.

------Index of Spanish Citizens Entering the Port of New Orleans between January 1840 to December 1865. New Orleans.

Villere, Sidney Louis. The Canary Island Migration to Louisiana, 1778-1783. Baltimore, 1972.

"Poblacion y Defensa de la Isla de Cuba, 1650-1700" in Anuario de Estudios Americanos. 44:1-87, 1987.

"Trabajo, Inmigracion y Colonizacion en Cuba, 1789-1847" in Siglo XIX, vol. 3, no. 6, 109-143.

Perez de la Riva, Juan. Demografia de los Culies Chinos,1853-74.La Habana, 1966.

Neasham, U.A. "Spain's Emigrants", Hispanic American Historical Review, vol. XIX, 147-160.

Perez Murillo, Maria Dolores. Aspectos Demograficos y Sociales de la Isla de Cuba en la Primera Mitad del Siglo XIX. Publicaciones de la Universidad de Cadiz.

Isern, J. Pioneros Cubanos en U.S.A., 1575-1898. Miami, 1971.

Crouse, Nellis M. French Pioneers in the West Indies, 1624-1664. Columbia University Press, New York, 1940.

Poyo, Gerald E. Cubans in Key West, 1868-1900. Austin, Texas.

Macias Dominguez, Isabelo. Cuba en la Primera Mitad del Siglo XVII. Imp.C.S.I.C., Sevilla, 1978.

Feyjoo Sotomayor, Urbano. Isla de Cuba. Inmigracion de Trabajadores Españoles. 1855.

Cifre de Loubriel, Estela. Catalogo de Extranjeros Residentes en Puerto Rico en el Siglo XIX. Ediciones de la Universidad de Puerto Rico,Rio Piedras, 1962.

Pasajeros a Nueva España, Filipinas, Peru, Buenos Aires, Islas de Barlovento...1516-1834. AGI, Indiferente General, legajos 2048-2107.

Relaciones de Pasajeros y Embarcaciones que van y vienen de Indias, 1563-1833. AGI, Indiferente General, legajos 2162-2172.

OFFICIAL RECORDS

The official printed records are those published by the Spanish or Cuban government which deal
with judicial matters,licenses, permits, admininis-
trations of estates, wills and many other legal matters.

These records are arranged chronologically and
divided by province, municipality and court. The
courts are divided into Courts of First Instance
(Primera Instancia), Correctional or Instructional
Courts and Municipal Courts. The Correctional and
Instructional Courts dealt with criminal cases and
the others mostly with civil cases.

In addition, there were the "Audiencias" which
dealt with either criminal or civil cases. The Sup-
reme Court was the court of last appeal and review.

If one knows the place and approximate time,it
is an easy task of getting the correct volume whose
pages may then be searched for the event in question.

These volumes also contain the various edicts
and decrees issued by the Crown,Captain General and
later the President and Assembly.

On the business end of life, the publication
had lists of trademarks and their owners, lists of
leftover merchandise at the various customshouses
throughout the island, lists of undeliverable letters and ecclesiastical concerns. After the inception of the republic, lists of registered voters
were published by places of residence. Although not
indexed, these volumes are not difficult to search
as long as the approximate time period is known.

During the colonial era,these are known as the
Gaceta de La Habana, though in the earliest years
the anme varied somewhat. Even though the title referred to La Habana, the content was island-wide.

Although gaps exist in the collections of the
various libraries in the United States which have
them, the ones with the most complete collections
are the Library of Congress, the University of Miami, Yale University (for the very early years) in

New Haven, Connecticut and the Boston Public Library. The BNC in La Habana has a complete run of all volumes.

The Gaceta de Puerto Principe was also published ever since the Audiencia de Santo Domingo was transferred there in 1800. This is similar in content to the Gaceta de La Habana and the New York Public Library has a very complete run of these for 1838 to 1843.

After Cuba was divided into six provinces in 1878, each provincial government began to publish its own official bulletin. These begin in 1879.

The BNC has a very complete collection of these. They are very similar in content to the Gacetas except that they are usually restricted to provincial matters. Some provinces did not publish theirs for very long.

Following is a list of the Boletines showing the dates of publication:

Boletin Oficial de la provincia de Pinar del Rio — 1879 to 1909.

Boletin Oficial de la provincia de La Habana — 1879 until 1959, at least.

Boletin Oficial de la provincia de Matanzas — 1879 to 1896.

Boletin Oficial de la provincia de Santa Clara — 1879 to 1899, approximately.

Boletin Oficial de la provincia de Puerto Principe (later Camaguey) — 1879 to undetermined if published still or when it stopped.

Boletin Oficial de la provincia de Oriente — 1879 until 1959, at least.

References

Quintero Mesa, Rosa. Latin American serials documents: A holding list. University Microfilms, Ann Arbor, Michigan, 1969.

SLAVE RECORDS

From the earliest days of Cuban colonization African slaves were probably introduced. Certainly, by 1511 some were imported to gather gold for the King of Spain.

By 1513, slave importation had definitely begun, but it was not until the economic upsurge and labor need caused by sugar and tobacco plantations that slaves were imported in large quantities. The largest number of slaves were imported during the 19th century when over one million were brought to the island.

There were two types of slave traffic. One was the legal one sanctioned by the Spanish Crown. The other was the illegal traffic which occurred at various times when the legal traffic was prohibited. Much of the illegal traffic took place as final abolition approached in 1886.

The records for the legal slave trade are in the AGI for the years 1584-1753. These are kept in section III with the "Contratacion" records. They are classified under "Registros de esclavos y de sus escrituras de compras" (slave registers and bills of sale).

The AHN in Madrid has the slave registration records for the years 1855 to 1859 in their "Ultramar" section in legajos 3547-3555. The Archivo del Consejo de Estado, also in Madrid, has in its section "Ultramar", subsection "Gobernacion", heading "esclavos y colonizacion" documentation relating to slaves and indentured servants.

In Cuba, many slave sale records may be found within the records of the different notaries in the ANC in the "protocolos" section. These records will usually give the date of sale, the seller, the purchaser, the slave's name, their African nation or tribe, their age and the sale price.

The ANC and the various municipal archives have saved thousands of purchase contracts plus many of the inventories from the sugar plantations or "ingenios". These inventories usually give the year of registration, the "ingenio" where each of the slaves resided or worked, the slave's name,age, sex, color, African nation or tribe, physical features, stature, moral character, health, occupation and purchase price.

The last major importation of slaves from Afrca took place between 1856 and 1863. After this, the various reguslations and laws passed restricted slave commerce more and more until its final abolition in 1886.

During the era of slavery, especially during the 19th century, most major newspapers throughout the island published lists of runaway slaves as well as advertisements for the sale of slaves. All lists varied, but most gave the name of the slaves, age, skill and any physical defects.

Slavery References

Moreno Fraginals, Manuel. "Africa in Cuba: A Quantitative Analysis of the African Population in the Island of Cuba" in Vera Rubin & Arthur Tuden (eds.), Comparative Perspectives on Slavery in New World Plantation Societies. New York 1977.

------El Ingenio. La Habana, 1978, 3 vols.

Perez de la Riva, Juan. El Barracon. Editorial Critica, Barcelona, 1978.

------El Monto de la Inmigracion Forzada en el Siglo XIX. Editorial de Ciencias Sociales, La Habana, 1979.

Corwin, Arthur F. Spain and the Abolition of Slavery in Cuba, 11817-1886. Austin, Texas, 1967.

Kiple, Kenneth F. Blacks in Colonial Cuba, 1774-1899. Gainesville, FL, 1976.

Saco, Jose Antonio. Historia de la Esclavitud. Ed. Alfa, La Habana, 2nd edition, 1936-45, 4 vols.

Vila Vilar, Enriqueta. Hispanoamerica y el comercio de esclavos. Escuela de los Estudios Hispanoamericanos, Sevilla, 1977.

Aimes, Hubert H.S. A History of Slavery in Cuba, 1511-1868. G.P. Putnam and Sons, New York, 1907.

Caballero, Jose Agustin. "Matrimonio entre Esclavos" in Escritos Literarios y Politicos. Universidad de La Habana, 1956.

Suarez Romero, Anselmo. El cementerio del Ingenio. 1863.

Franco, Jose Luciano. Comercio Clandestino de Esclavos. Editorial Ciencias Sociales, La Habana, 1980.

Alcala Hanke, Agustin. La esclavitud de los negros en la America espanola. Madrid, 1919.

Perez Landa, R. "Los Palenques en Cuba" in Nuevos Mundos, no. 5, October 1947.

Ortiz, Fernando. Los Negros Esclavos. Editorial de Ciencias Sociales, La Habana, 1976.

One should not ignore newspapers as a source of vital statistics, passenger arrival and departure information as well as obituaries. In addition, commercial information, advertisements and news may give valuable clues toward locating an ancestor.

The "Diario de la Marina" was continuously published in La Habana from 1832 until 1960. Between 1832 and 1844 it was known as "El Noticioso y Lucero de La Habana". Prior to its merging in 1832, "El Noticioso" had been published since 1813.

The "Diario" is easily accessible in the United States by interlibrary loan. For years, the issues from 1899 to 1960 have been available on microfilm. As of this writing, the microfilming for the earlier years was well under way at the Library of Congress.

As with most Cuban newspapers available in the United States, the "Diario" has a gap of 1882 to 1899. Only a few scattered issues are found in any of the American repositories. One has to look to the BNC for any of these missing issues.

Although in its early years they were not as prevalent, this newspaper is full of obituaries and small notices about deaths. Although they are mostly for people who died in La Habana, many appear for those who died in other Cuban cities and towns as well as foreign countries.

Cuban obituaries are most useful because they usually include a long list of relatives, in-laws and friends. Additionally, prior to the popular usage of funeral homes, the body was prepared and laid for viewing in the home of the deceased. For this reason, the obituary contained the address of the house where the funeral was being held. This is extremely helpful in locating the church which the deceased probably attended and where the death record may be found.

At the turn of the century, the "Diario" began publishing daily lists of deaths in La Habana. The lists were divided according to "barrios" and, later, civil registry districts. These lists usually contained the name of the deceased, place of birth, cause of death, place of death given either as the home address of the deceased or the name of the hospital or clinic where the death occurred and the person's race. Although not as frequently published, lists of deaths from other parts of Cuba were printed in a section called "Necrologia".

Additionally,the names of those people married by a civil ceremony were published by "barrios" or civil registry district. The only information given besides their name was their race. However, most marriages were not shown because most people continued to marry by the Catholic Curch until 1918 when civil marriages became compulsory even if a church ceremony took place.

Other newspapers in La Habana and other major Cuban cities regularly published the same type of information as the "Diario". However, due to their limited accessibility, either because they are not available in the United States, Spain or England or are not on microfilm,one has to rely to a great extent on the "Diario de la Marina".

Passenger Records

In most of the issues of the "Diario", from its inception until the 1910s, lists of passengers of arriving and departing vessels were published. Although nothing but the passengers' names were shown, these are very useful for determining a person's approximate place of origin. Knowing the port of departure may lead one to locate other documents indicating the place of birth or residence.

Moreover, once an arrival date has been determined, then the proper records in Cuba may be inspected without wasting time searching irrelevant or incorrect documentation. These published lists usually included those in first and second class, but those in third class have not been completely ignored.

When searching American records about someone from Cuba,these published lists may lead one to the corresponding American passenger arrival lists. For the port of New York City, this is especially helpful since no index exists for the passenger lists between 1847-1896. Also, since many of the American lists have been lost, these newspaper lists serve in lieu of those no longer in existence. This is especially helpful for minor ports such as Key West and Tampa in Florida.

For Key West, there is a gap in the lists from 1869-1897 and for Tampa there are no lists at during this period and after. Both of these ports were traditional ports of destination for many Cubans, especially during the Ten Years' War of 1868-1878 and the War of Independence of 1895-98. So any newspaper list for those periods is very valuable.

Equally so, American newspapers should not be neglected for this purpose. The New York Herald, New York Tribune, Charleston (SC) Daily Courier, Boston Transcript and many other newspapers in the United States regularly published arriving and departing passenger lists from their ports to anywhere in the world.

Although these newspapers have not, for the most part, been indexed, in lieu of lost or destroyed official lists, they are of immense value as a starting point.

As air travel came into vogue in Cuba during the 1920s, airplane passenger lists were published in Cuban newspapers. As the newsness wore off, these were discontinued.

Other Records

Other valuable sources in Cuban newspapers include sections such as "Sociales", "Matanceras", and other reports from localities throughout the island which the "Diario" and most other newspapers published daily or weekly. These were social in nature, but not limited to the upper classes.

Lists of undeliverable letters were regularly published so that the addressees would be able to obtain them. At times lists of people, mostly Spaniards, who had become Cuban citizens appeared in the newspapers. Lengthy lists of people who made charitable contributions and the names of society individuals who had attended very elegant parties would appear from time to time.

If one had an ancestor involved in legal matters during the early to mid-20th century, it may
be useful to search through the sections of the
newspapers which listed the different proceedings
taking place in the various courts of La Habana. In
similar fashion, newspapers from other cities and
towns would print the same type of information for
their particular localities.

A couple of guides to the location of Cuban
newspapers in the United States are the Latin American Newspapers in U.S. Libraries: A Union List by
Steven Charno published in 1968 and Newspapers in
Microform-Foreign Countries 1948-1983 published by
the Library of Congress in 1984.

The AHN and Biblioteca Nacional in Madrid both
have collections of Cuban newspapers and pamphlets,
especially from last century. The difficulty in
accessing these, however, lies in their being mixed
with other as yet uncatalogued documentation.

Cuban Newspapers Available in the U.S.

"Pinar del Rio"
        La Fraternidad 1883-98
        El Comercio 1871-77 (DLC)

"Isla de Pinos"
        Isles of Pines Appeal 1904-13 (DLC)

"La Habana"
        Diario de la Marina 1832-1960 (DLC,CU)
        La Prensa de La Habana 1841-70 (DLC)
        La Voz de Cuba 1868-88 (possibly 1882) (DLC)
        Boletin Comercial 1861-96 (MB)
        La Discusion 1887-1937 (DLC,FU)
        Havana Post 1900-60 (DLC,CU)
        La Lucha 1885-1930 (DLC,FU,NN,NcU)
        El Mundo 1901-60s (DLC,CU,CSt-H,FMU,FU)
        Havana Weekly Report 1823-90s (DLC,MB)

"Matanzas"
        Aurora del Yumuri 1828-1900 (DLC)

"Cardenas"
        Boletin Mercantil (DLC)

58

"Cienfuegos"
La Correspondencia 1898-1940s (DLC)

"Camagüey"
El Camagüeyano 1900-54 (DLC)

"Santiago de Cuba"
El Cubano Libre 1895-1910s (DLC,MH)

The years listed are those for which each was published and for which the listed depository may have some or all of it.

The above list is but a partial representation of the Cuban newspapers available in the United States. One should write for a detailed list of the holdings of each newspaper at each depository if one does not locate these newspapers in the above-mentioned guides.

The Biblioteca Nacional "Jose Marti" has the largest and most complete collection of Cuban news-papers. Some of the titles, for example,are available in their entirety. For a very complete listing see Teresita Batista Villarreal's Catalogo de Publicaciones Periodicas Cubanas published in La Habana in 1965.

Newspapers Published by Cubans in the U.S.

Due to the many Cuban migrations which have occurred as a result of political turmoil on the island during the last 150 years, many different newspapers have been published by Cubans in the United States.

Many of these were political in nature, how-ever, some such as "El Yara" published from 1869 to 1876 and "El Republicano" published from 1878-1899 contain much information useful to genealogists. Both of these were published in Key West, Florida. Others include:

"New York"

    La Cronica 1848-67
    El Cronista 1867-77
    El Cubano 1852-54
    La Independencia 1873-80

59

"Tampa"

Cuba 1893-98

These are all available in the BNC. Some of them are available in the Library of Congress and the New York Public Library.

Other useful material may be found in Francisco Mota's <u>Para la Historia del Periodismo en Cuba: Un Aporte Bibliografico</u> published in 1985 by Editorial Oriente in Santiago de Cuba. In addition, Carlos Tamayo Rodriguez published "Notas para el estudio de las publicaciones periodicas en Santiago de Cuba,1900-1930" in the journal <u>Santiago</u> 49:125-159, March, 1983.

References

Peraza Sarausa, Fermin & Elena Verez. <u>Directorio de Revistas y Periodicos de Cuba.</u> Cuba, 1940s and Florida, 1968.

Garcia Carranza, Araceli. <u>Indice analitico de la Revista Bimestre Cubana.</u>

The following is a list of some periodicals available in the Library of Congress:

Cuba y America 1897-1917
Cuba Contemporanea 1913-1927
Revista Bimestre Cubana 1831-34, 1910-51
La Revista de Cuba 1877-84
Revista Cubana 1935-57

COMMERCIAL RECORDS

Not until the late 18th century were Spanish laws liberalized enough to allow Cuba relatively free commerce with other nations besides Spain.

According to the "Informe del Gobernador Jose DE GALVEZ al Conde de Florida Blanca" dated 10 May 1875, the English and American merchants who lived in La Habana were: David BECERIDGE (dealer in salted meat), Joseph GRAPHETON, Alexander SAMPLET, John MILLER, Thomas PLUNKET, Robert TOTEN, Robert DORCI, George CHANDLER, George C. MORTON and Vincent GRAY.

The records of the "Real Consulado y Junta de Fomento de la Isla de Cuba, 1795-1854" housed in the ANC contain records which deal with commerce and industry among other subjects. A brief index was published in the Boletin, volume I, numbers 1-4.

A later publication deals in much more detail with this section of the ANC. The work is volume I of the ANC's Publicaciones dated 1943. It is titled "Catalogo de los Fondos del Real Consulado de Agricultura, Industria y Comercio de la Junta de Fomento". It has an index of names of people and places.

Beginning in 1900, the law required all merchants or businessmen to register with the authorities. This "Registro de Comerciantes" was kept at the "Registro Mercantil" of the capital of each province. The required items were: names and surnames of the merchant, age, civil status, type of business, name of business, business location and branches and starting date. For infornmation on see OFFICIAL RECORDS.

References

Rodriguez Ferrer, Miguel. El Tabaco; su historia, cutlivo, sus vicisitudes, sus afamadas vegas en Cuba..., Madrid, 1851.

Rivero, Jose. Tabaco, su Historia en Cuba. Instituto de Historia, La Habana, 1965.

Museo Postal Cubano. <u>Desarrollo del Correo Interior de Cuba y sus Marcas Postales, 1765-1877.</u> Cuadernos del Museo Postal Cubano,La Habana,1974.

-----<u>Desarrollo del Correo Exterior de Cuba y sus Marcas Postales, 1765-1877.</u> Cuadernos del Museo Postal Cubano, La Habana, 1973.

Porter, Robert Percival. <u>Report of Commercial and Industrial Conditions of Cuba.</u> 1976.

Marrero, Levi. <u>Cuba, Economia y Sociedad.</u> Madrid, 1972-88, 14 volumes.

Friedlander, H.E. <u>Historia Economica de Cuba.</u>1944.

The following are some business or economic periodicals available at the Library of Congress:

Cuba Review 1902-31
Bulletin 1902-31
Gaceta Economica 1902-43?
Boletin Informativo 1952-58
Revista Oficial del Ministerio de Comercio
Diario de la Importacion 1919-1960

MILITARY RECORDS

Military records of interest to those researching Cuban ancestors would primarily be found in Spain with the smaller portion located in Cuba.

Many of the forces in Cuba known as "voluntarios" (volunteers) were composed by Spaniards who volunteered for the purpose of migrating to Cuba. After their service many of these individuals invariably remained in Cuba. They became the heads of later Cuban families and some even sided with the Cuban insurrectionists during the various wars and rebellions.

Spanish Records

Records of Spanish army officers from the 18th century are housed by the Servicio Historico Militar of the Archivo General Militar in Segovia. By writing to this archive, one may be able to obtain copies of records found under "hojas de servicio" or service sheets and "expedientes personales" or personal files, if the soldier was an officer. When making a request one should provide the name of the soldier, place of service, time period and unit, if it is known.

Alternatively, one may search the published 9-volume index titled, Archivo General Militar de Segovia: Indice de Expedientes Personales by Vicente de Cadenas y Vicent. These volumes were published in Madrid by Ediciones Hidalguia between 1959 and 1963. The volume contents are as follow:

Volume	From-To
1	A-Blum
2	Bo-Chy
3	D-Garces
4	Garci-H
5	I-Mazzini
6	Meabe-Pereyra
7	Perez-Samuel
8	San Agustin-Vazquez Vega
9	Vea-Zuzuarregui

Once located, these records may be a wealth of

information providing, not only the name of the officer, but also the date and place of birth, names
of parents and the name of the wife, if married.

The Archivo de Simancas has a published index
to its "hojas de servicio de America" (records of
service in America) which date from the late 18th
to early 19th centuries. These include Cuba and
are primarily for officers. The LDS Family History
Library has some for Cuba on microfilm as follow:

Years	Microfilm No.
1765,1786-88	1156324
1789-90	1156325
1791-92	1156326
1793-95	1156327
1796-97	1156328
1798-1800	1156329

The records for the enlisted soldier will be
found under "filiaciones" or "hojas de filiacion".
These regimental registers will give the researcher
the name of the soldier, his parents, birthplace,
place of residence, religion, marital status and a
physical description. These are not usually indexed, so one needs to provide as much information as
possible when writing to the archive.

Similarly, naval records may be obtained from
the Archivo Central de La Marina or Museo Naval.
Due to the lack of printed finding aids, naval records are much more difficult to locate. The Archivo de Simancas should also be contacted as they
have a section "de La Marina" with records from the
year 1711 to 1784.

Cuban Records

The vast amount of information refers mostly
to the Ten Years' War (Guerra de los Diez Años)1868
to 1878 and the War of Independence (Guerra de la
Independencia) 1895 to 1898. This last war is known
in the United States as the Spanish-American War.

The ANC has in its historical collection the
Archivo de Roloff, 1895-1898 which was gathered by
Carlos Roloff. These are the records he used to
write his monumental work, Indice Alfabetico y De-

funciones del Ejercito Libertador de Cuba.

This volume provides information about the individuals who were members of the Cuban insurrectionist army. It not only provides the names of the army members, but for some their age and parents' names are also given. Additionally, it contains a list of those killed in action along with the details of how their deaths occurred, when and where.

Seleceted issues of the Gaceta Oficial de la Republica de Cuba published lists of those who had applied or were eligible for pensions based on military service during the War of Independence. These lists were published within three to four years after the Cuban Republic was born on 20 May 1902.

However, even in 1917, there were still thousands of claims pending and which were periodically published in the Gaceta. Since wives and children of veterans were eligible, a great deal of burden was put upon the financing of the pension system. The Cuban government conyemplated removing descendants from the eligible list in order to help ease the financial burden.

A list of foreigners in the Cuban Army of Liberation was published by Jorge Quintana in 1953. The book was titled, Indice de Extranjeros en el Ejercito Libertador de Cuba, 1895-98. Many of the names are those of Americans who had been fighting on the Cuban side long before the United States entered the war.

Also of interest is the publication by the ANC titled, Inventario General del Archivo de la Delegacion de Partido Revolucionario Cubano en Nueva York, 1892-1898. Though this collection consists mostly of letters of a political nature,many people are mentioned who ultimately served in the Cuban Army.

Other military records of enlisted men may be located in the various provincial and municipal archives of Cuba.

References

Ribo, Jose Joaquin. Historia de los Voluntarios Cubanos, 1872-1876. 2 volumes.

Otero Pimentel, Luis. Memoria de los Voluntarios de
ls Isla de Cuba. 1876.

Registro de documentacion de Cuba, Puerto Rico, y
Filipinas para el Archivo Historico Militar de
Madrid. Negociado de Ultramar, Madrid.

Rodriguez Exposito, Cesar. Indice de medicos, den-
tistas, farmaceuticos y estudiantes en la Guerra de los Diez Años. La Habana, 1968.

Ejercito de Ultramar en Cuba: Infanteria y Caba-
lleria: escalafon general de los Sres. jefes
oficiales y sargentos primeros de dichas armas
y milicias...1863,1864,1865,1866. Imp.Militar,
Madrid.

Ocerin, Enrique de. Indice de los expedientes ma-
trimoniales de militares y marinos, 1761-1865.
Madrid, 1959.

Pirala, Antonio. Anales de la Guerra de Cuba. 1895.

Guillen, Julio F. Indice de los expedientes y papeles de la seccion de Indiferente del Archivo Central de La Marina. Madrid, 1951.

Guerra Sanchez,Ramiro.Guerra de los Diez Años,1868-
1878. Cultural S.A., La Habana, 1952.

66

U.S.DEPARTMENT OF STATE RECORDS

Since the Department of State iis the one cab-
inet department which handles the foreign affairs
of the United States, then among its records one
may locate records of American consulates in Cuba.
Also, any record generated by contact with the Spanish , and later, Cuban legations in Washington,
D.C. will be found in the Department's holdings.
Most of these records are kept at the National Archives of the United States and are available on microfilm as follow:

Diplomatic Despatches, microfilm #T158, 18 rolls.
Diplomatic Instructions of the Department of State,
    1801-1906,microfilm #M77-Cuba 1902-06,roll 49.
Notes to Foreign Legations in the United States
    from th Department of State, 1834-1906, M99-
    Cuba 1902-06, roll 17; Spain 1834-1906, rolls
    85-90.
Notes from Foreign Legations in the United States
    to the Department of State, Cuba 1844-1906,
    T800, 2 rolls.
Notes from the Spanish Legation to the Department
    of State, 1790-1906, M59, 31 rolls.

. These records cover mostly matters of state
and politics, but if one's ancestors were involved,
then these records may lead to others more informa-
tive newspaper articles or documents. The records
prior to 1902 are with the Spanish Legation papers.

The records of the despatches sent by the var-
ious American consulates in Cuba are found in the
Despatches Received by the Department of State from
U.S. Consuls in:

Baracoa, 1878-99, T511, 3 rolls.
Cardenas 1843-5 & 1879-98, T583, 5 rolls.
Cienfuegos, 1876-1906, T548, 8 rolls.
Havana, 1783-1906, T20, 133 rolls.
Manzanillo, 1844-6, T613, 1 roll.
Matanzas, 1820-99, T339, 17 rolls.
Nuevitas, 1842-7 & 1892-8, T588, 1 roll.
Puerto Principe & Jibara, 1828-43,T567,1 roll.
Sagua la Grande, 1878-1900, T678, 6 rolls.
San Juan de los Remedios, 1844-6,T584,2 rolls.
Santiago de Cuba, 1799-1906, T55, 17 rolls.
Trinidad, 1824-76, T699, 9 rolls.

Though most of these records involved routine commercial matters as well as replies to inquiries from the Department of State, there are quite a number of documents related to Americans living on the island, their deaths, disposition of their property and other claims made during time of war.

Records of the American Embassy in La Habana (Diplomatic Post Records) are found in the National Archives Record Group (RG) 84, Records of Foreign Serrvice Posts of the Department of State. For Cuba between 1902-1935, there are 126 feet of diplomatic records and 18 volumes of diplomatic despatches for 1902-1906.

The actual everyday records of the various consulates are as follow:

Antilla (including Jibara & Banes), 1903-46.
Baracoa, 1905-23, 3 ft.
Caibarien, 1903-43, 16 ft.
Camagüey, 1915-8 & 1941-9, 4 ft.
Cardenas, 1869-1924, 12 ft.
Cienfuegos, 1865-1945, 66 ft.
Guantanamo (including Caimanera), 1898,1904-6,
    & 1914-8, 4 ft.
Havana, 1820-1935, 230 ft.
Manzanillo, 1905-49, 7 ft.
Matanzas, 1857-1943, 38 ft.
Nueva Gerona (including Santa Fe), 1904-28 &
    1942-4, 14 ft.
Nuevitas, 1905-48, 55 ft.
Sagua la Grande, 1876-98, 5 ft.
Santiago de Cuba, 1819-1958, 71 ft.
Trinidad, 1856-98, 2 ft.

Notice how there are consular records from places from which there no despatches. This is due to the fact that some cosulates sent their despatches through the Havana Consulate, as is the case with those from Camaguey and Manzanillo. The National Archives has prepared preliminary inventory lists for some of these American records.

Although most of the records deal with everyday commercial transactions, some are of much genealogical valu. The miscellaneous record books for Havana contain reports of the deaths of American citizens, copies of wills of American, reports of the births of children of Americans and more for

the years 1878 to 1934. Additionally, there are
registers of American citizens, their wives and
children, passport applications, passport records,
visas and many other records.

The Department of State has amassed many other
documents which could be of genealogical value depending on the record,time period and circumstances.
For a more complete description of these one should
consult the <u>Guide to Materials on Latin America in
the National Archives</u> by George S.Ulibarri and John
P.Harrison published in 1974.

<u>References</u>

Schneider, Philip F.(comp.). <u>Preliminary Inventory
of the Records of the U.S.Consulate General in
Havana, Cuba.</u> RG 84, General Services Administration, Washington, D.C., 1956.

Jorgensen, Margareth (comp.). <u>Preliminary Inventory
of the Records of the Military Government of
of Cuba.</u> PI 145, National Archives & Records
Service, Washington, D.C., 1962.

Rieder, Roland and Charlotte M. Ashby (comps.).<u>Pre-
liminary Inventory of the Records of the Provisional Government of Cuba.</u> PI 146, National
Archives & Records Service, Washington, D.C.,
1962.

Munden, Kenneth. <u>Records of the Bureau of Insular
Affairs Relating to the U.S. Military Government of Cuba, 1899-1902 and the U.S. Provisional Government of Cuba, 1906-09.</u> SL3, 1943.

CONSULAR RECORDS

Cuban Consular Records

The available Cuban consular records were acquired and microfilmed by the University of Texas at Austin. These records are for the Consulate at Key West, Florida. Although some of the documents relate to routine consular business, many are of great genealogical value. The records are as follow:

Birth, marriage and death registrations, 1886-1952.
Notary (protocolos) records, 1903-51;with index, 1903-49.
Register of Cuban citizens, 1912-38 with an index for records prior to 1912 and post 1938.
Records of Cuban ships arriving at Key West, 1904-60.
Register of requisitional letters (from one judge to another), 1904-51.
Passport register, 1918-50.

These records are available within the Nettie Lee Benson Latin American collection of the University of Texas at Austin or the LDS Family History Library on microfilm. Many of the records, especially the Register of Cuban Citizens, contain copies of other documents such as baptism, birth and marriage certificates.

Spanish Consular Records

Spanish consular records for the consulates at Charleston, South Carolina and Savannah, Georgia are available at the manuscript department of the William R. Perkins Library of Duke University in Durham, NC.

The documentation covers the period from 1794 to 1898 with gaps. The principal material of concern to genealogists are the 45 bound volumes which contain passport registers log books, crew lists for the period of 1861-67 and 1868-71 for Charleston and 1850-60 for Savannah. This is an especially important period because it covers the American Civil War and part of the Cuban Ten Years' War.

Most of the other records deal with routine consular matters, but a large portion relates to the activities of Cuban revolutionaries and filibustering expeditions.

For records of the Spanish consulates at Key West, New York City or New Orleans, through which many Cubans passed, are located within the Archivo del Ministerio de Asuntos Exteriores in Madrid.

All these foreign affairs documents prior to 1900 are available for research. The important collection of the archive is the one called "Ultramar" contained in lagajos 2900-2951 covering the period from 1824 to 1900.

A guide to this archive was published in 1981 by Jose M. Lozano Rincon. It is titled, Guia del Archivo del Ministerio de Asuntos Exteriores.

French Consular Records

After the Haitian Revolution at the end of the 18th century, many French refugees migrated to Cuba and settled along the eastern tip of the island. After their eviction from Cuba in March 1808, many of them immigrated to the United States. A great many became Spanish citizens and remained in Cuba.

The material available from the French consulates is the United States are made up of registers of those who arrived and their subsequent affairs. The documentation also includes some records prior to the Haitian Revolution.

The following records are available from the LDS Family History Library in Salt Lake City on microfilm:

     Surname index, A-K, microfilm #960760
     Surname index, L-Z, # 960761
     Charleston, SC records, 1750-1804, #960766
     Charleston, SC records, 1805-26, #960767
     New York City, 1793-98, #960768
     Norfolk, VA, 1752-1814, #960768
     New Orleans, 1803-21, #960768
     Philadelphia, 1789-97, #960769; 1798-1801,
                   #960770; 1802-11, #960771.

Related to the above records is a collection
of papers from Baracoa, Cuba and Santiago de Cuba
dealing with French refugees from Haiti. The correspondence covers the priod from 1804 to 1808 in
Baracoa and 1803 to 1809 in Santiago de Cuba. These
are also available from the LDS on microfilm.

For records of the French Consulate at·La Habana, one may wish to write to the Ministere des
Affaires Exterieures, Archives Diplomatiques, salle
266, 37 quai d'Orsay, 75007 Paris, France.

British Consular Records

Many different records are available from the
British consulates in Cuba. These are kept by the
Public Record Office in London under Foreign Office
records in the subdivision of Embassy and Consular
Archives and then either under Spain or Cuba. The
Guide to the Contents of the Public Record Office
published in two volumes in London in 1963 will be
a great help in determining their reference numbers.

Also of value is the Guide to Sources in Brit-
ain for the History of Latin America and the West
Indies. This was published by Clarendon Press in
London.

CEMETERY RECORDS

Cemetery records are a valuable source of information. Many of those for La Habana were published last century and are available in book form or microfilm. This is especially important for the Espada Cemetery in La Habana which was closed in 1868. This cemetery, also known as the "Cementerio General", was subsequently demolished after the removal of the burials. The remains of those whose bodies were not reclaimed were removed to an ossuary in the new cemetery.

The Colon Cemetery became the new cemetery and was much larger and further away from the center of the city. For many years in a section titled, "Cementerio de Colon", the "Diario de la Marina" published questions and answers from readers regarding the moving of their loved ones and other cemetery concerns.

In September of 1919, the burial charges were as follow:

Private vaults	$10.00	(pesos)
Temporary burial		
Adults	$ 5.30	"
Children	$ 4.25	"
Exhumations	$ 4.50	"
Certificates	$ 1.00	"

The prices for the cemetery plots varied from ten pesos per meter in the common ground to thirty pesos in the first class area. Immediately adjacent to the Colon Cemetery is the Protestant Cemetery. A few blocks away, the Chinese Cemetery is located.

Various other cemeteries have served the city of La Habana throughout its history. The "Cementerio del Vedado" which functioned from 1832 until 1847 was sued as a slave burial place. The better section was used to bury foreign Protestants and so and so the cemetery came to be called the English Cemetery.

The "Cementerio del Cerro" was in use from 1817 to 1860. All the burials in this cemetery were made in the ground without any vaults or niches.

The Jesus del Monte Cemetery, located behind the church of its name, was in use from at least 1848 to 1860.

Two other cemeteries were provisionally opened to handle the very large mortality which occurred during the cholera epidemics of 1833 and 1850. The first was the "Cementerio de los Molinos" located on the hillside of Principe Castle and the second the "Cementerio de Atares" located on the slopes of Atares Castle. This last one was in use until 1868.

Two very important works were published listing the burials in the Espada and Colon cemeteries. The first was published by Pujola y Cia. at the time of the closing of the Espada Cemetery in 1868. It is titled <u>Guia del Cementerio de La Habana</u>. It is a somewhat alphabetical work which contains approximately 7,000 names. These usually have the date of death as well as their burial location within the cemetery.

Even of more value because of their thorough nature are the three volumes published by Domingo Rosain between 1874 and 1876. These volumes dealt with the vault burials of the Espada Cemetery in the first volume, its niches in the second and the third onlt with the Colon Cemetery. They are titled <u>Necropolis de La Habana</u>.

As with La Habana, most other cities and towns in Cuba started out by having their cemeteries as part of their church yards. However, due to the rapid growth of the population in some places and the sometimes unsanitary conditions which prevailed, most places soon enough built separate cemeteries. For a valuable work on some of these see Fernando Fernandez Escobio's <u>Raices Cubanas, Iglesias y Camposantos Coloniales</u> published in Miami in 1991.

References

Stanislas, Andres. <u>La Necropolis de La Habana. Catalogo completo de las personas inhumadas en bovedas y los nichos del Cementerio General.</u> La Habana, 1867.

Florida Genealogical Society. <u>Hillsborough County, Florida Cemeteries.</u> Several volumes, Tampa, FL.

Smith, Leonard H. Jr. <u>Key West Cemetery, 1889-1905.</u>

Gonzalez del Valle, Ambrosio. <u>Tablas Obituarias de Cuba.</u> La Habana, 1872 and others.

Llaverias, Joaquin. <u>Historia de los Archivos de Cuba.</u> La Habana, 1912.

Zapata Casanova, Felipe. <u>Catalogo Sumario de los Fondos Existentes en el Archivo Nacional.</u> La Habana, 1958.

MISCELLANEOUS RECORDS

Archivo Nacional de Cuba

Obviously,many different records housed in the Archivo Nacional de Cuba are very useful to the genealogical researcher. Following is but a small sample of the lesser known ones:

Section	Record
Florida Oriental	Registro de puertos,roles,guias y memoriales pidiendo pasaportes-legajo 136 (passports).
Capitanias Generales	Salvador de Muro,Marques de Someruelos, 1799-1812: emigrados de Santo Domingo-legajo 645. Juan Ruiz de Apodaca, 1812-16: matrimonios-lejago 786, Pasaportes-legajo 813 (marriages & passports). Jose Cienfuegos, 1816-19: Pasaportes-legajo 874.
Licencias de Fabricas	Construction permits indexed by first surname.
Policia	Passports to move from one location to another, 1800-81-legajos 1324-1420.
Ministerio de Estado	Eighty-four volumes of "Registro de Españoles (register of Spanish citizens) who wanted to remain Spanish citizens after Cuban independence.

Other available records are: "Dispensas de Matrimonios", 1812-79-legajos 888-935. These records relate to the right to contract marriage of couples not having the consent of their parents or guardians. Also, there are "Libros de Matriculas de La Habana",1818-9-legajo 5478. These pertain to taxes.

The "Registro de Servicio Domestico"was a register of people who were hired as domestic workers. During 1879-80,the workers had to register with the authorities in the city hall in their locality.

Universidad de La Habana

The Universidad de La Habana has a surname index to its collection of "expedientes antiguos". These files relate mainly to the applications to the University and the requirement of proving that applicant was of clean blood. This is referred to as "limpieza de sangre".

These documents contain much valuable genealogical information since the applicants had to provide "family trees" in detail which would show that they or their families were not mixed or descended from black, Indian or Jewish blood. In other words, the applicants had to be of "Spanish" blood or descent. These records need to be used with caution since many of them were contrived.

Manuscript Records

One needs to consult the National Union Catalog of Manuscript Collections and its yearly supplements to determine all the libraries and repositories which may have manuscript records pertaining to Cuba.

A cursory glance through these volumes shows that many papers exist pertaining to Cuba which were collected by individuals who in one way or another had dealings with Cuba. Many merchants' papers are available which may contain useful data.

The Library of Congress' Manuscripts on Microfilm is also a useful finding aid. In addition, the article by Ernest J. Burrus, S.J. titled,"An Introduction to Bibliographical Tools in Spanish Archives and Manuscript Collection to Hispanic America", is a very useful guide for Spanish archives' manuscript collections. This was published in the Hispanic American Historical Review for November 1955.

References

Archivo General de Indias. Catalogo de Documentos de la Seccion Novena. Volume-1 Santo Domingo, Cuba, Puerto Rico, Luisiana, Florida and Mexico. Sevilla, 1949.

Schafer, E. Indice de la Coleccion de Documentos de Inidas. 1946-7, 2 vols.

Griffin, A.P.G. List of Books Relating to Cuba. Library of Congress, Washington, D.C., 1898.

Cuba, Coleccion de Folletos. Biblioteca Nacional, Madrid, Spain.

Gomez Canedo, Lino. Los Archivos de la Historia de America - Periodo Colonial Español. 2 vols., 1961.

Index to Official Published Documents Relating to Cuba and the Insular Possessions of the United States, 1876-1906. Microfilm #M24, 3 rolls.

Instituto Hispano-cubano de Historia de America. Publicaciones. Catalogo de los Fondos Cubanos del Archivo General de Indias. Sevilla, 1935.

Marino Perez, Luis. Guide to the Materials for Amrican History in Cuban Archives. Washington, D.C., 1907.

Direccion General de Archivos y Bibliotecas. Guia de Fuentes para la Historia de Ibero-america conservadas en Espana. Madrid, vol. 1-1966 & vol.2-1969.

Hill, Roscoe R. Los Archivos Nacionales de la America Latina. Publicaciones del Archivo Nacional de Cuba.

Moreno Freginals, Manuel. Misiones cubanas en los archivos europeos. Mexico, 1951.

Walne, Peter. A Guide to Manuscript Sources for the History of Latin America and the Caribbean in the British Isles. London, 1973.

Torres de Mendoza, Luis. Coleccion de documentos ineditos, relativos al descubrimiento, conquista, y organizacion de las antiguas posesiones... Imp. de J.M. Pérez, Madrid, 1869.

Biblioteca Nacional (Madrid). Inventario General de Manuscritos de la Biblioteca Nacional. Madrid, 1953.

Addresses of Cuban Archives and Libraries

Archivo Nacional de Cuba
C.Compostela y San Isidro
C. Habana, Cuba

Casa de las Americas(books)
G y 3a., Vedado
C. Habana, Cuba

Universidad de La Habana
Biblioteca General
San Lazaro y L
C. Habana, Cuba

Biblioteca Municipal de
    La Habana
Neptuno 817
C. Habana, Cuba

Casa de Beneficencia y
    Maternidad
San Lazaro esq.P.Varela
C. Habana, Cuba

Academia de la Historia
    de Cuba
Amargura 157
C. Habana, Cuba

Biblioteca Nacional
"Jose Marti"
Plaza de la Revolucion
C. Habana, Cuba

Oficina del Historiador
    de la Ciudad
Museo de La Habana
Palacio de los Capitanes
    Generales
Plaza de Armas
C. Habana, Cuba

Universidad Central de
    Las Villas
Biblioteca General
Santa Clara, Cuba

Biblioteca Publica
    "Gener y Del Monte"
Independencia 17
Matanzas, Cuba

Universidad de Oriente
Biblioteca General
Santiago de Cuba, Cuba

U.S. Book Dealers

Ediciones Universal
P.O. Box 450353
Miami, FL 33245-0353

La Moderna Poesia
5246-5250 SW 8th St.
Miami, FL 33134

Libros Latinos
P.O. Box 1103
Redlands, Ca 92373

Saeta Ediciones
P.O. Box 440156
Miami, FL 33144

DIRECTORIES

The most useful secondary source material for locating people are the many city, provincial and commercial directories published in Cuba from the 18th to the 20th centuries.

Their primary value lies in allowing the genealogist to pinpoint an individual to a specific place and era. This information may then be used to locate primary records.

A secondary value of the directories is that, at times, familial relationships can be established when two or more people are listed under one address even with different surnames. This is especially true if the address contains a single-family dwelling.

The earliest of these directories is the <u>Calendario Manual y Guia de Forasteros de la Siempre Fiel Isla de Cuba</u> which began publication in 1791. It lists the names and titles of the administrative personnel as well as those of the military and ecclesisatic authorities. In addition, lawyers, university professors and dcotors are also listed. A few of those listed are given with their address.

Besides the BNC and the Biblioteca del Ayuntamiento de La Habana, there are a few other repositories with very complete collections. These include the British Museum Library,Biblioteca Nacional in Madrid, the Library of Congress,the Peabody Institute in Baltimore, Harvard University, Yale University, the University of Florida,the University of California at Los Angeles and many others.

The following is a list of some of the directories available and where they might be located:

Directorio de la Ciudad de La Habana y Estramuros, 1840,41,42. (DLC,NN)
Directorio de Artes, Comercio e Industrias de La Habana, 1859, 60. (DLC,NN)
Almanaque Mercantil, 1863-80. Biblioteca Nacional, Madrid; Harvard University.
Directorio General y Comercial de La Habana e Isla de Cuba, 1874. (2nd year) (NN)
Directorio de Matanzas, 1900,2,3,4,13.

Directorio Hispanoamericano: Septimo Ano,ano econo-
mico 1879-80. (University of California,Davis)
Guia Comercial de la Isla de Cuba,1886,7,1902,3,18-
24. (Biblioteca Nacional, Madrid.
Directorio Mercantil de la Isla de Cuba, 1891.(3rd
year) (DLC)
Directorio General de la Republica de Cuba, 1901,4,
5,7-8. (DLC)
Guia Directorio de la Republica de Cuba, 1912, 20.
(DLC)
Anuario de la America Latina, 1920-21. (3rd year)
(DLC)
Directory of Havana and Commercial Handbook of Cuba
for 1899. (DLC)
Directorio General para 1883-4, 1884-5, de la Isla
de Cuba. (DLC)
Directory of the Tobacco Industry of the United
States and Havana, Cuba, 1887. (DLC)
Commercial Directory of Cuba and Puerto Rico. Bur-
eau of the American Republics, Bulletin no.38,
March 1892. (DLC)
Commercial Directory of the American Republics.
International Bureau of the American Republics
Bulletin no. 91, 1898. (DLC)
Directorio de Cuba, 1927. (DLC)
Libro de Oro de la Sociedad Cubana, 1917? (DLC)
Directorio Comercial e Industrial Cubano, 1951, 52.
(UCLA)
Directorio Comercial del Municipio de La Habana,
1954. (DLC).
Directorio de Abogados, 1953,6-9. (DLC)
Anglo-American Directory of Cuba, 1960. (DLC)
Delmar's Classified Business Directory of Mexico,
Central and South America and Cuba, 1887. (NN)
Directorio de la Provincia de Santiago de Cuba,1889
1890. (CU)
Directorio Social de La Habana, 1944,5,8,54-9.(DLC,
NN)
Directorio Social de Cuba, 1919. (DLC,CU)
Anuario Social de La Habana, 1937. (4th year)(DLC)
Primer Anuario Medico-social de Cuba, 1937. (DLC)
Directory of the Officials of the Republic of Cuba,
1984. (various libraries)
Directorio Medico de Cuba, 1906,7,8,9,16. (Natio-
Library of Medicine, Washington, D.C.)
Directorio Oficial de Exportacion e Importacion,
Produccion y Turismo, 1940s. (DLC)
Anuario de Familias Cubanas, 1971-2,73-4,88 by Joa-
quin de Posada. (various libraries)

PAPELES PROCEDENTES DE CUBA

These "papeles" are a collection of copies of papers and documents relating to colonial Cuba. The majority of them are positive photostatic copies with some typewritten copies. These were copied at the AGI during the 1930s.

The majority are for the period which covers the second half of the 18th through the first half of the 19th centuries. The entire collection was photographed in legajo sequence. Two reels of microfilm which accompany the collection are impossible to read because of bad filming and poor originals.

Besides colonial Cuba, these documents refer to the surrounding colonies of Louisiana, Florida and other Caribbean islands. They also include many descriptions of North American Indians. Since many, if not most of the Spanish colonists living in these places migrated to Cuba as the colonies were lost by Spain, the researcher may want to check these papers for references to their ancestors.

References

Hill, Roscoe. A Descriptive Catalogue of the Documents Relating to the History of the U.S. in the Archivo General de Indias at Seville..., Carnegie Institution, Washington, D.C., 1916.

Coutts, Brian E. An Inventory of Sources in the Department of Archives and Manuscripts, Louisiana State University for the History of Spanish West Florida. Louisiana History, XIX, Spring 1978, 213-50.

Historical Records Survey. List of the Papeles Procedentes de Cuba in the Archives of the North Carolina Historical Commission. Raleigh, 1942.

Beers, Henry Putney. French and Spanish Records of Louisiana. A Bibliographic Guide to Archive and Manuscript Sources. Louisiana State University Press, Baton Rouge & London, 1988.

CUBAN GENEALOGICAL SOCIETIES & SOCIAL CLUBS

The Instituto Cubano de Genealogia y Heraldica was founded in La Habana in 1950. It began publishing a newsletter, Correo, in June of 1957. The newsletter was published quarterly until the Instituto was disbanded after the CASTRO takeover. The newsletter was good for historical settings and the origins of some surnames, though its main concern was the nobility.

Also in existence was the Academia Cubana de Ciencias Genealogicas. It published a Boletin Oficial.

There has not been a great amount published about Cuban genealogy or family histories. However, what has been published is quite good, though again it is mostly about families with a noble or wealthy background. The refernce section of this chapter has a listing of these.

Since 1988, the Cuban Genealogical Society has been in existence in Salt Lake City. It publishes a quarterly newsletter called, Revista. This publication so far deals mostly with the publication of indexes of the abstracts made the Conde de Jaruco and his colleagues for his publication, Historia de Familias Cubanas published in the 1940s.

Other artciles have appeared on different subjects such as land records, family histories, commercial houses and other matters. A query section is included most of the time. Their complete address is: Cuban Genealogical Society, P.O. Box 2650, Salt Lake City, Utah 84110-2650.

Throughout Cuban history, there have been several instances where political turmoil and war have caused a large migration of Cubans to the United States and other nations. These Cuban exiles began many organizations and clubs mostly in New York, Tampa, Key West and more recently New Jersey, Chicago, New Orleans,California and many other places.

Though the majority of these clubs have been concerned with political matters, they always had a social side to them. Many have published a newsletter in which articles of historical significance have been presented. Additionally, many published lists of their members and their birthdays or wedding anniversaries. Obituaries also have appeared from time to time. Some of them have printed old photographs of school groups in Cuba identifying the people in them.

A few of the clubs and societies which existed in New York City towards the end of the 19th century are as follow:

> Socieded de Laborantes Cubanos founded 1868
> Cuban Benevolent Society of N.Y.   "   1874
> Cuban Giant Baseball Exhibition   "   1888
> Cuban Orphan Society   "   1900

These are but a few of those found within the records of the County Clerk's certificates of incorporation. Whether any records for these exist, is presently unknown. A thorough search of the local historical societies and libraries may prove fruitful.

The LDS Family History Library has on microfilm the records of the "Circulo Cubano" in Tampa. Besides the name of the member, other information is also given.

Some of the associations in existence in Key West from the late 1860s until the end of the 19th century were: Club Patriotico Cubano, Asociacion Patrotica Cubana, Ateneo Democratico Cubano, Asociacion Patriotica del Sur and Obreros de La Libertad.

The most recent wave of exiles has brought many new societies into existence. Some of these are:

> Municipio de Bolondron   Publishes "El Reloj"
>   en el Exilio
> P.O. Box 350398
> Miami, FL 33135

> Municipio de Matanzas   Publishes "El Matan-
>   en el Exilio   cero Libre"
> 904 SW 23rd Ave.
> Miami, FL 33135

> Municipio de Cienfuegos
> 2140 W. Flagler St.
> Miami, FL 33135

Municipio de Puerto Padre
2150 W.10th Ave.
Hialeah, FL 33010

Cofradia Ntra.Sra.de la   Publishes "Boletin
   Caridad del Cobre   Oficial"
P.O. Box 454
South Gate, CA 90280

Genealogical References

Nieto Cortadellas, Rafael. Los Fernandez de Cossio. Imp.de la Universidad de La Habana, 1955.

-----"Indice de varios linajes portugueses establecidos en Cuba" in Revista Genealogica Latina, año 1950, no. 2, Sao Paulo, Brazil.

-----Dignidades Nobiliarias en Cuba. Madrid, 1954.

-----Genealogias Habaneras. "Hidalguia", Madrid, 1979-80, 2 vols.

Vallellano, Conde de. Nobiliario Cubano-Las Grandes Familias Isleñas. Madrid, 2 vols., n.d.

Bustamante, Luis Jorge. Diccionario Biografico de Cienfuegos. 1931.

Calcagno, Francisco. Diccionario Biografico Cubano. New York, 1878.

Ludwigs, Emil. Biografia de Una Isla (Cuba). 1948.

Castro de Cardenas, Fernando R. de. Genealogia,Heraldica e Historia de Nuestras Familias. Ediciones Universal, Miami, 1989.

Rodriguez, Emilio. Familias Hispanoamericanas.

Cuartas, Augusto. Apellidos Catalanes - Heraldica de Catalunya. Paraninfo, S.A., Madrid, 1987.

Santa Cruz Mallen, Francisco X. Historia de Familias Cubanas. La Habana and Miami, several years, 9 vols.

Diccionario Biografico del Poder Judicial de Cuba. 1936.

Peraza Sarausa, Fermin. Diccionario Biografico Cu-
    bano. Cuba, 1951 and Gainesville, FL, 1965,
    14 vols.

-----Personalidades Cubanas. Cuba, 1957 and Gaines-
    ville, FL, 1964-8, 10 vols.

Montoto, Santiago. Nobiliario Hispanoamericano del
    Siglo XVI.

MAPS AND ATLASES

Many sources for Cuban maps of all sizes and scales exist. The gamut runs from the early maps available from the AGI to tourist maps recently published.

One of the best sources for maps of La Habana are the several volumes of the <u>Reports of the Military Government of Cuba, 1899-1902.</u> These maps were updated versions of the maps made by Esteban T. Pichardo in 1873. He made various maps of La Habana, other Cuban cities and all the provinces.

Since these maps were made in large scale format, the detail shown is astounding. The province maps not only show the names of the "ingenios" and their boundaries, but they also show the names of individual "hatos" and "estancias". These are available at the Library of Congress and the Instituto Geografico y Catastral, C. General Ibañez Ibero #3, Madrid, Spain.

The Provisional Government of Cuba, 1906-1909 remapped Cuba and also made maps of many cities and towns. These are available at the National Archives of the United States.

Cultura, S.A. published maps of the provinces showing judicial divisions as well as municipal boundaries in 1932. These also show the names of the sugar plantations and other small farms. Again, they are housed in the Library of Congress.

In 1957-9, the Instituto Cubano de Cartografia y Cadastro published a set of maps for all the provinces including Isla de Pinos with a 1:200,000 scale except for Matanzas. The Library of Congress is the main repository for these outside of Cuba.

These updated those made in 1932 by the Estado Mayor del Ejercito and known as the "Carta Militar de la Republica de Cuba. The scale for the earlier ones is 1:100,000 and were printed in 25 sheets as follow: Pinar del Rio-sheets 1-10,13; La Habana-11, 12,14-6,19; Matanzas-18,21,22,24,25; Las Villas-17, 20,23. There were none made for the provinces of Camagüey and Oriente.

In 1952 and 1953, many "municipio" maps were prepared by the Instituto Cartografico Nacional and the Oficina de los Censos Demografico y Electoral. In 1957, they were republished with a scale varying from 1:20,000 to 1:60,000. Almost all of then existing 126 municipios were mapped.

Cuba is presently divided into thirteen provinces and one free-standing "municipio" as follow:

From west to east-Pinar del Rio, La Habana, Matanzas, Villa Clara, Cienfuegos, Sancti Spiritus, Ciego de Avila, Camagüey, Las Tunas, Holguin, Granma, Santiago de Cuba and Guantanamo. Isla de Pinos is a "municipio" unto itself with no provincial affiliations.

References

Chueca Goiti, Fernando. Planos de Ciudades Iberoamericanas y Filipinas existentes en el Archivo General de Indias. Instituto de Estudios de Administracion Local, 1951.

Pichardo, Esteban T.Caminos de la Isla de Cuba.Itinerarios. Imp.Militar de M.Soler, La Habana, 1865, 3 vols.

-----Geografia de la Isla de Cuba. 1854, 4 vols.

Freyre, Joaquin.Historia de los Municipios de Cuba. Miami, 1985.

Ministerio de Asuntos Exteriores de Espana.La Habana Vieja. Mapas y Planos en los archivos de España. 1986.

Marquez, Jose de J. Diccionario Geografico de la Isla de Cuba. Imp. Perez, Sierra y Cia., reprint of 1875 edition, La Habana, 1926.

Cien Planos de La Habana en los Archivos Espanoles. 1985.

Pezuela, Jacobo de la. Diccionario Geografico, Estadistico, Historico de la Isla de Cuba. Imp. de Mellado, Madrid, 1863-66, 4 vols.

Alcedo A.de. <u>Diccionario Geograficohistorico de las Indias Occidentales o America.</u> 1789, 5 vols.

Bernardo Estrada, Rodrigo de. <u>Manual de Agrimensura Cubana.</u> 1854.

Herrera, Desiderio. <u>Agrimensura Aplicada al Sistema de Medidas de la Isla de Cuba.</u>

Calderon Quijano,Jose A. <u>Guia de los documentos,mapas y planos sobre historia de America.</u> 1962.

Figarola Caneda, Domingo. <u>Cartografia Cubana del British Museum,Catalogo Cronologico de Cartas, Planos y Mapas de los Siglos XVI al XIX.</u>La Habana, 1910.

Sagra, Ramon de la. <u>Historia fisica, politica y natural de la Isla de Cuba.</u> Paris, 1842-61, 12 vols.

-----<u>Historia economico-politica y estadistica de Isla de Cuba.</u> La Habana, 1831.

Erenchun, Felix. <u>Anales de la Isla de Cuba; diccionario administrativo, economico, estadistico y legislativo.</u> La Habana, 1861-5, 5 vols.

Cancela, Pedro. <u>Geografia maritima de la Isla de la Isla de Cuba.</u> La Habana, 1951.

STREETS, "BARRIOS" & DISTRICTS OF LA HABANA

The streets of La Habana as with other Cuban cities and towns acquired their names through popular usage. Over the course of history the street names have been changed many times. However, some were so popular and in use for such a long time that even when they changed the people continued to call them by their old names. One of the best references regarding street anmes and their history is Las Calles de La Habana Intramuros by Manuel Fernandez Santalices. It was published in Miami in 1989.

In 1922, the Gaceta Oficial de la Republica de Cuba published the old and new street names of La Habana and the date thay changed.This list follows:

Old Name	New Name	Date
Ancha del Norte (also San Lazaro)	Ave.de la Republica	6 Dec 1909
Amistad	Miguel Aldama	23 Apr 1903
Aguila	Rafael M.de Labra	16 Feb 1912
Animas	General Aguirre	25 Aug 1920
Alcantarilla	Dr.Ruiz de Luzuriaga	18 May 1921
Amargura	Marta Abreu	16 Dec 1921
Aguacate	Perfecto Lacoste	16 Dec 1921
Bomba	Progreso	22 May 1899
B.Lagueruela	Pedro Consuegra	13 May 1910
Belascoain	Padre Varela	13 Dec 1911
Bernaza	Placido	17 Apr 1912
Blanquizal	Benavides	17 Mar 1915
Consulado	Estrada Palma	19 Jun 1902
Correa	Ave.Presidente Gomez	8 Jan 1909
Concordia	Enrique Villuendas	16 Feb 1910
Campanario	General Aranguren	4 Sep 1916
Cristina	Ave. de Mexico	25 Nov 1921
Carcel	Capitan Cepdevila	2 Jan 1922
Dolores	Jesus Rabi	21 Jan 1916
Division	Cowley	8 Aug 1921
Egido	Ave. de Belgica	20 Nov 1918
Empedrado	General Riva	18 May 1921
Estrella	Barnet	8 Aug 1921
General Ena	Narciso Lopez	3 May 1904
Galiano	Ave. de Italia	28 Noc 1917
Hospital-Carnero	Gen.Freyre de Andrade	27 Apr 1921
Jovellar	26 de Noviembre	26 Nov 1903
Jesus Peregrino	Nestor Sardiñas	10 Jan 1912

Jesus del Monte	Ave. 10 de Octubre	9 Oct	1918
Lagueruela	Jose M. Heredia	6 Jan	1911
Linea or Nueve	Ave.Presidente Wilson	22 Nov	1918
Lealtad	Martin Morua Delgado	27 Apr	1921
Luyano	Manuel Fdez.de Castro	18 May	1921
Municipio	Manuel de la Cruz	19 May	1904
Gutierrez de la Vaga	Ayesteran	12 Dec	1904
Marina	Coloma	17 Nov	1905
Malecon	Ave. Antonio Maceo	6 Dec	1909
Maloja	Francisco V.Aguilera	17 Jan	1910
Marques de La Habana	Felipe Poey	6 Jan	1911
Madrid	Francisco Polanco	24 Aug	1917
Monserrate	Ave. de Belgica	28 Oct	1918
Neptuno	Zenea	9 Oct	1918
Obispo	Pi y Margall	27 Mar	1905
O'Reilly	Presidente Zayas	27 Apr	1921
Paseo de Tacon (also Carlos III)	Ave.de la Independencia	7 May	1902
Calzada del Monte (also Principe Alfonso)	Maximo Gomez	19 Jun	1902
Principe de Asturias	Primelles	25 Nov	1910
Prado	Paseo de Marti	7 Nov	1904
Pocito	Fernando Quiñones	18 May	1921
Reina	Simon Bolivar	9 Oct	1918
Revillagigedo	Gen.Quintin Banderas	18 May	1921
Samaritana	Porvenir	22 May	1899
Sevilla	Artes	17 Nov	1905
Santo Tomas	Damas	7 Apr	1913
Santa Marta	Antonio Diaz	21 Jan	1914
San Jose	Jose de San Martin	13 Aug	1920
San Rafael	General Carrillo	18 May	1921
San Miguel	Gen.Manuel Suarez	16 Dec	1921
Tacon	Teodoro Roosevelt	6 Jan	1920
Trocadero	America Arias	15 Jun	1921
Virtudes	Mayor Gorgas	25 Aug	1920
Infanta	Ave.del Pres.Menocal	27 Apr	1921
Zulueta	Ignacio Agramonte	22 Mar	1909
Zanja	Finlay	24 Mar	1916
San Cayetano	San Nicolas	n/a	

Some of these streets are outside of La Habana proper in the "barrios" or neighborhoods of Cerro, Jesus del Monte, Casa Blanca, Vedado, Vivanco and Acosta. Equally so,many other cities and towns have gone through various changes for their street names and these may be found in some of the town histories found in GENERAL REFERENCES.

Municipal Districts & "Barrios" of La Habana-1858

Intramuros (inside city wall)

First District	Second District
Templete	San Francisco
San Felipe	Santa Clara
Santo Cristo	Santa Teresa
San Juan de Dios	Paula
Santo Angel	San Isidro

Extramuros (outside city wall)

Third District	Fourth District
Tacon	Arsenal
Colon	Jesus Maria
La Punta	La Ceiba
Guadalupe	Vives
Monserrate	San Nicolas
Dragones	Marte
San Leopoldo	Chavez
San Lazaro	Peñalver
	Pueblo Nuevo

Fifth District	Six District
Atares	(Regla—across the
Pilar	bay)
Villanueva	Sanctuario
Jesus del Monte	Cementerio
Cerro	
Principe	
Arroyo Apolo	

In 1900, the city was divided into six electoral districts. In addition, four Municipal Courts and Courts of First Instance (Primera Instancia) were formed. The street boundaries for these may be located in the Report of the Military Governor of Cuba.

Boundaries of "Barrios" in La Habana-1900

Templete - On O'Reilly from the harbor west to San Ignacio, south to Teniente Rey or San Salvador, east to harbor.
San Felipe - From San Ignacio west on O'Reilly to

Compostela, south to Teniente Rey, east to San
Ignacio, north to point of origin.

Santo Cristo - From Compostela west on O'Reilly to
Monserrate, south to Teniente Rey, east to Compostela, north to point of origin.

San Juan de Dios - On O'Reilly from harbor, west to
Habana, north to Monserrate, north to harbor.

Santo Angel - From Habana west on O'Reilly to Monserrate, north to Habana, south to point of
origin.

Casa Blanca - across the bay.

San Francisco - From harbor west on Acosta to San
Ignacio, north to San Salvador or Teniente Rey,
east to harbor.

Santa Clara - From San Ignacio west on Acosta to
Compostela, north to Teniente Rey, east to San
Ignacio, south to point of origin.

Santa Teresa - From Compostela west on Acosta to
Egido/Monserrate, north to Teniente Rey, east
to Compostela, south to point of origin.

Paula - From harbor west on Acosta to Egido, south
to Desamparados/harbor.

San Isidro - From Habana west on Acosta to Egido,
south to Desamparados/harbor.

La Punta - From waterfront south on Monserrate to
Trocadero, west to Galiano, north to waterfront.

Colon - From Monserrate west on Trocadero to Galiano, south to San Rafael, east to Monserrate,
north to point of origin.

Tacon - From Monserrate west on San Rafael to Galiano, south to Vapor, east to Prado, north to
Dragones, east to Monserrate/Plaza del Sol,
north to point of origin.

Marte - From reina south on Manrique to sitios, east
to Los Angeles, south to Monte/Principe Alfonso, east to Plaza del Sol/Monserrate, north to
Dragones, west to Prado, south to Vapor/Reina,
west to point of origin.

Monserrate - From waterfront south on Galiano to
San Miguel, west to Lealtad, north to waterfront.

Dragones - From Galiano west on San Rafael to Lealtad, south to Reina, east to Galiano, north to
point of origin.

Guadalupe - From Lealtad west on San Miguel to Belascoain, south to reina, east to point of origin.

San Leopoldo - From waterfront south on Belascoain
to San Miguel, east to Lealtad, north to water.

Arsenal – From Factoria south on Monte/Principe Alfonso to the bay, east to Plaza del Sol/Egido,
   south to bay.
Ceiba – From Principe Alfonso south on Factoria to
   Esperanza, west to Aguila, north to Mision,
   west to Florida, north to Los Angeles, north
   after a right to left zig-zag to Monte, east
   to point of origin.
Jesus Maria – From bay north on Factoria to Esperanza, west to Florida, south to Diaria, west
   to Alambique, south to the bay.
Vives – From the bay north to Diaria, east to Florida, north to Gloria, west to Figuras, south
   to the bay.
San Nicolas – From Gloria west on Figuras to Manrique, north to Sitios, east to Los Angeles,
   south to Gloria, west to point of origin.
Peñalver – From Manrique west on Figuras to Belascoain, north to reina, east to Manrique, south
   to point of origin.

References

Cartas, Francisco. Recopilacion historica y estadistica de la jurisdiccion de la Habana por
   distritos... La Habana, 1856.

"Plazas y Paseos de La Habana Colonial" in Arquitectura, XI, 1943.

Barras Prado, Antonio de las. La Habana a mediados
   del Siglo XIX. Madrid, 1925.

Fuentes, Walfrido & Alejandro Valenzuela (eds.).
   Habana, plano monumental de la ciudad y guia
   general. Imp.Rambla, Bouza y Cia., La Habana,
   1927.

Perez Beato, Manuel. La Habana Antigua. Editorial
   Seoane y Fernandez, La Habana, 1936.

Sanchez Agusti, Maria. Edificios Publicos de La Habana en el Siglo XVIII. Universidad de Valla-
   dolid, 1954.

Weiss, Joaquin E. La Arquitectura Colonial Cubana.
   volume I-16th & 17th centuries; volume II-18th
   century. Editorial Letras Cubanas, La Habana,
   1979.

GENERAL REFERENCES

Colegio de Abogados de La Habana. Lista de los Abogados del Colegio de La Habana con expresion
del numero de antiguedad y sus domicilios:1885
Estab.Tip.de Soler,Alvarez y Cia., La Habana,
1885.

Roig de Leuchsenring, Emilio. Medicos y medicina en
Cuba. La Habana, 1965.

Llaca Argudin, Francisco. Organizacion de los Tri-
bunales de Cuba y su personal,1899-1922.La Habana, 1923.

Quintero Almeyda, Jose M. Apuntes para la Historia
de la Isla de Cuba con relacion a la ciudad de
Matanzas desde el año 1695 al 1877. Imp.El Fe-
rrocarril, Matanzas, 1878.

Varona, Esteban A. de. Trinidad de Cuba. Editorial Alfa, La Habana, 1946.

Martinez Escobar, Manuel. Historia de Remedios.Imp.
Publicitas, La Habana, 1944.

Cuevas Morillo, Ernesto de las. Baracoa ante la
Historia. Imp. La Cronica, Baracoa, 1925.

Martinez Arango, Felipe. Proceres de Santiago de
Cuba. Imp.de la Universidad de La Habana,1946.

Pino, M. del. Apuntes para la Historia de los Hos-
pitales en Cuba, 1523-1899. La Habana, 1963.

Guerra, Ramiro. Historia de la Nacion Cubana. La
Habana, 1952, 10 vols.

Avila Delmonte, Diego de. Memoria sobre el origen
y fundacion del hato de San Isidoro de Holguin
1865.

Bayle, Constantino. Los Cabildos Seculares en la
America Espanola. 1952.

Perez Luna,Rafael.Historia de Sancti Spiritus.1888.

Borah,Woodrow.La demografia historica de la America
Latina:fuentes,tecnicas,controversias...,1972.

Torres Lasqueti, Juan. Coleccion de datos histori-
cogeograficos de Puerto Principe y su jurisdiccion. La Habana, 1907.

Perez, Luis M. Apuntes de libros impresos en España y en el extranjero que tratan expresamente
de Cuba desde principios del siglo XVII hasta
1812. La Habana, 1907.

Diaz-Trechuelo Espinola, Maria L. "La despoblacion
de la Isla de Canaria y la emigracion ilegal a
Indias, 1621-1625" in Actas del I Coloquio...,
1976.

Baez, Vicente (ed.) La Enciclopedia de Cuba. Madrid, 1974, 9 vols.

Pariseau, Earl J. (comp. & ed.). Cuban Acquisitions
and Bibliography. Library of Congress, Washington, D.C., 1970.

Ryskamp, George R. Tracing your Hispanic Heritage.
Riverside, California, 1984.

Wright, Irene A. Santiago de Cuba and Its District,
1607-1640.

Valle, Adrain del. Indice de las Memorias de la Sociedad Economica de Amigos del Pais,1793-1896.
Molina y Cia., La Habana, 1938, 2 vols.

Edo Llop, Enrique. Memoria Historica de Cienfuegos
y su Jurisdiccion. Cienfuegos, 1888.

Bacardi Moreau, Emilio. Cronicas de Santiago de Cuba. La Habana, 1908, 10 vols.

Trelles, Carlos M. Biblioteca Historica Cubana. Matanzas, 1922-24, 3 vols.

Primelles, Leo. Cronica Cubana,1915-18 and 1919-22.
La Habana, 1955.

Pogolotti, Marcelo. El Caseron del Cerro. La Universidad de Las Villas, La Habana, 1961.

Alfonso, Pedro Antonio. Memorias de un Matancero.
Matanzas, 1854.

Maceo Verdecia, Jose. Bayamo. Manzanillo.

Oliva Pulgaron, Luis. **Apuntes Historicos sobre la Masoneria Cubana.** La Habana, 1934.

Quintero, Jose Mauricio. **Apuntes Historicos de Matanzas.** Matanzas, 1881.

Vivanco Diaz, Julian. **Estampas Antiguas de San Antonio de los Baños.** La Habana, 1948-9.

Prince, J.C. **Guidebook and General Information of Havana, Matanzas and the Island of Cuba, 1885-6** Moss, New York, 1885.

Reynolds, Charles B. **Standard Guide to Cuba.** Foster and Reynolds, New York, 1905.

Mena, Cesar. **Historia de la Odontologia en Cuba.** Miami, 1984, 4 vols.

Orovio, Helio. **Diccionario de la Musica Cubana.** La Habana, 1981.

Le Roy Cassa, J. **La Primera Epidemia de Fiebre Amarilla en La Habana en 1649.** La Habana, 1930.

Vidal Cirera, Felix. **Historia de la Villa de Guanabacoa.** Imp. La Universal, La Habana, 1887.

Instituto del Libro. **Indice Historico de la Provincia de Camagüey, 1899-1952.** La Habana, 1970.

Bachiller Morales, Antonio. **Apuntes para la historia de las letras y de la instrucccion publica en la Isla de Cuba.** La Habana, 1965, 2 vols.

Humboldt, Baron A. de. **La isla de Cuba, ensayo politico.** 1827.

Pichardo Vinals, Hortensia. **La Fundacion de las Primeras Villas de la Isla de Cuba.** Editorial de Ciencias Sociales, La Habana, 1986.

Inglis, Gordon D. **Historical Demography of Cuba.**

Roldan Oliarte, Esteban (ed.) **Cuba en las mano. Enciclopedia popular ilustrada.** Imp. Ucar, Garcia y Cia., La Habana, 1940.

Buch Lopez, Ernesto. **Historia de Santiago de Cuba.** Editorial Lex, La Habana, 1947.

Castellanos, Gerardo. Trinidad, la secular y revolucionaria. La Habana, 1942.

Castellanos, Jose F. Trinidad: Biografia de un Pueblo. Laurenty Publishing Inc., Miami, 1989.

Garcia Chavez, Leonardo. Historia de la jurisdiccion de Cardenas. Cultural, S.A., La Habana, 1930.

Hellberg, Carlos. Historia estadistica de Cardenas, 1893-1957. Comite Pro-calles de Cardenas,1957.

Cruz del Pino, Mary. Camagüey (Biografia de una provincia). Academia de la Historia de Cuba, La Habana, 1955.

Valdes, Antonio J. Historia de ls Isla de Cuba y en especial de La Habana.

Varona Pupo, Ricardo. Banes.Cronicas. Santiago de Cuba, 1930.

Figarola Caneda, Domingo. Diccionario Cubano de seudonimos. Imp.El Siglo XX, 1922.

Tanco, Felix. Los jesuitas en La Habana. Philadelphia, 1862.

Anuario Azucarero de Cuba. 1937-60.

INDEX

103